BEAD FANTASIES IV

THE ULTIMATE COLLECTION OF BEAUTIFUL, EASY-TO-MAKE JEWELRY

SAMEJIMA Takako

JAPAN PUBLICATIONS TRADING CO., LTD.

TABLE OF CONTENTS

READ THIS BEFORE YOU BEGIN A PROJECT.

☆If your vendor doesn't carry the designer or gemstone beads specified in this book, feel free to substitute beads of the same size and shape.

☆In our list of supplies for each project, we sometimes specify the manufacturers of a particular type of bead. T stands for Toho and M for Miyuki. Gemstone beads, being natural objects, vary in size. Sizes given in this book are meant to serve as guidelines.

☆We include approximate lengths for nylon thread and wire. Since the holes in gemstone beads are traditionally very small, we recommend using thin (0.205mm diameter) nylon thread.

☆In the drawings, we indicate the starting point with a ★ symbol, and the ending point with a ☽ symbol.

©2004 by Takako Samejima

Translated by Connie Prener

©2006 English tex., Japan Publications Trading Co., Ltd.
English edition by Japan Publications Trading Co.,Ltd. 1-2-1, Sarugaku-cho, Chiyoda-ku, Tokyo 101-0064, Japan

Original Japanese edition published by Nihon Bungei-sha Co., Ltd., 1-7 Kanda Jinbo-cho, Chiyoda-ku, Tokyo 101-8407, Japan.

First edition, First printing : July 2006
        Second printing : November 2006

Distributors:
United States: Kodansha America, Inc. through Oxford University Press, 198 Madison Avenue, New York, NY 10016.
Canada: Fitzhenry & White Side Ltd., 195 All States Parkway, Ontario, L3R 4T8.
Australia and New Zealand: Bookwise International Pty Ltd. 174 Cormack Road, Wingfield, SA 5013, Australia.
Asia and other countries: Japan Publications Trading Co., Ltd., 1-2-1, Sarugaku-cho, Chiyoda-ku, Tokyo 101-0064, Japan.

ISBN-13: 978-4-88996-204-8
ISBN-10: 4-88996-204-2

Printed in Japan

Part 1

SPECIAL-OCCASION PIECES

Gemstones lend an air of luxury and elegance to any piece of jewelry. The eight design styles in this section, created with very special occasions in mind, take that luxury and elegance one step further. Gold, silver and black accents add sophistication.

Nostalgic Style

We used matte gemstones in these designs to evoke days gone by. Tiny rose motifs and shell-shaped metal beads add touches of refinement.

Rose Necklace & Ring

Button coral beads form the petals of the rose motifs in these pieces. Three of the motifs adorn the bright necklace. We added extra petals to the rose on the matching ring.

Instructions: p. 6

Shell Necklace & Earrings

The mother-of-pearl beads give
the gold shell beads a natural look.
The coral and aventurine beads
add a feminine note.

Instructions, p.

Nostalgic Style

ROSE NECKLACE & RING

Finished length (necklace): 41cm
Motif diameter: 1.5cm (small motif), 2cm (large motif)

● Supplies (Necklace)

Round red agate beads (136 2-mm beads, 30 4-mm beads)
Coral beads (40 2-mm round beads, 58 1 x 6-mm button beads)
40 2-mm seed beads (red: M309)
2 crimp beads
Spring clasp
Adjustable chain closure
3 70-cm lengths nylon thread
60cm nylon-coated wire

1

Make small motif, beginning by stringing 6 red agate beads on center of nylon thread to form a circle. Add more beads, referring to drawing and photo.

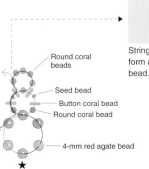

String coral and seed beads; form an intersection in a coral bead.

- Round coral beads
- Seed bead
- Button coral bead
- Round coral bead
- 4-mm red agate bead

★

2

Repeat the figure eight pattern. Once you've passed the thread through the first red agate beads strung once more, tie threads together and finish off. Note: The large motif is made in the same way, except that you begin with 8 red agate beads, and make 8 petals.

- Seed bead
- Round coral bead
- Button coral bead
- Red agate bead strung in Step 1

3

String motifs and beads on nylon-coated wire. Add a crimp bead at each end of necklace. Attach clasp to one end and adjustable chain closure to other.

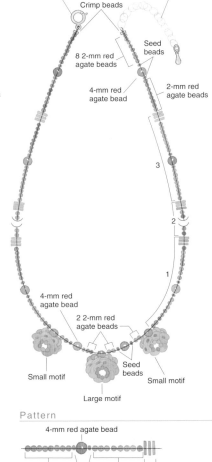

- Clasp
- Crimp beads
- Adjustable chain closure
- 8 2-mm red agate beads
- Seed beads
- 4-mm red agate bead
- 2-mm red agate beads
- 3
- 2
- 1
- 4-mm red agate bead
- 2 2-mm red agate beads
- Seed beads
- Small motif
- Large motif
- Small motif

Pattern

- 4-mm red agate bead
- 8 2-mm red agate beads
- 8 2-mm red agate beads
- Seed beads
- 3 button coral beads

Approximate size: 6 1/2
Motif diameter: 2cm

● Supplies (Ring)

Round red agate beads (10 2-mm beads, 19 4-mm beads)
Coral beads (24 2-mm round beads, 24 1 x 6-mm button beads)
16 2-mm seed beads (red: M309)
Nylon thread (1 40-cm length, 1 90-cm length)

Referring to Steps 1-2 of instructions for necklace, make a motif with 12 petals, using 90cm nylon thread. With 40cm thread, pick up a red agate bead on motif and weave band. Tie threads together and finish off.

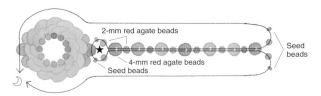

- 2-mm red agate beads
- Seed beads
- 4-mm red agate beads
- Seed beads
- ★

SHELL NECKLACE & EARRINGS

Finished length (necklace): 63cm

● Supplies (Necklace)

43 4.5 x 6-mm teardrop mother-of-pearl beads (white)
9 7-mm round coral beads
42 2-mm round howlite beads
6 10 x 20-mm oval red aventurine beads
20 2-mm round metal beads
2 11.5 x 17-mm shell-shaped designer drops (gold)
1 9 x 30-mm shell-shaped designer drop (gold)
4-mm Swarovski bicone crystal beads
(6 aurum gold 2X, 14 white alabaster)
4 2-cm eyepins
2 crimp beads
Spring clasp
Adjustable chain closure
80cm nylon-coated wire

1

Make necklace components.

2

String necklace components and beads on nylon-coated wire. Add a crimp bead at each end of necklace. Attach clasp to one end and adjustable chain closure to other.

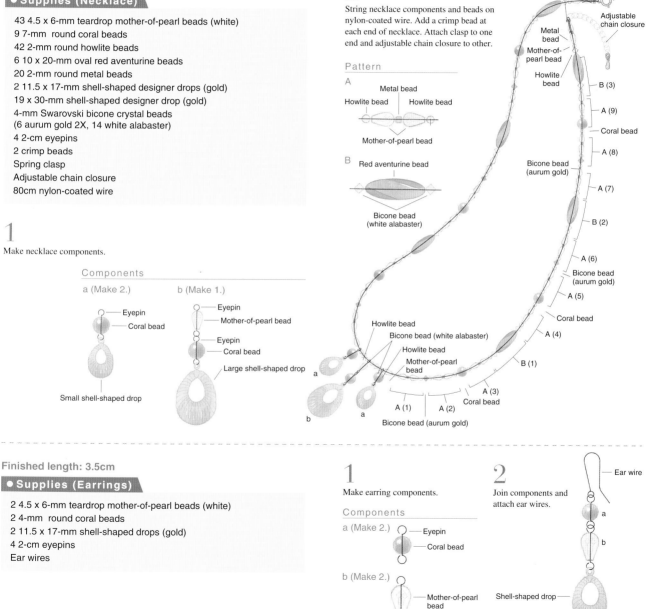

Pattern

A

Metal bead
Howlite bead — Howlite bead
Mother-of-pearl bead

B

Red aventurine bead
Bicone bead (white alabaster)

Components

a (Make 2.)
Eyepin
Coral bead
Small shell-shaped drop

b (Make 1.)
Eyepin
Mother-of-pearl bead
Eyepin
Coral bead
Large shell-shaped drop

Crimp bead
Clasp
Adjustable chain closure
Metal bead
Mother-of-pearl bead
Howlite bead
B (3)
A (9)
Coral bead
A (8)
Bicone bead (aurum gold)
A (7)
B (2)
A (6)
Bicone bead (aurum gold)
A (5)
Coral bead
A (4)
B (1)
A (3)
Coral bead
A (2)
A (1)
Bicone bead (aurum gold)
Howlite bead
Bicone bead (white alabaster)
Howlite bead
Mother-of-pearl bead

Finished length: 3.5cm

● Supplies (Earrings)

2 4.5 x 6-mm teardrop mother-of-pearl beads (white)
2 4-mm round coral beads
2 11.5 x 17-mm shell-shaped drops (gold)
4 2-cm eyepins
Ear wires

1

Make earring components.

Components

a (Make 2.)
Eyepin
Coral bead

b (Make 2.)
Mother-of-pearl bead
Eyepin

2

Join components and attach ear wires.

Ear wire
a
b
Shell-shaped drop

ANTIQUE STYLE

When you add touches of gold to a bright color scheme, it takes on an antique look. Simple designs have a sophisticated impact.

Art Deco Necklace & Ring

The color scheme is unmistakably Art Deco: black, green and coral. We have modernized these pieces by keeping the motif small.

Instructions: p. 10

Ball Necklace & Earrings

Interspersing gold rings and metal beads with gemstone beads gives these easy-to-make pieces a ravishing look. Freshwater pearl beads in two colors are subtle touches.

Instructions: p. 11

ART DECO NECKLACE & RING

Finished length (necklace): 43cm
Motif diameter: 2cm

● Supplies (Necklace)

Round onyx beads (96 2-mm beads, 18 3-mm beads, 12 4-mm beads)
Round turquoise beads (32 3-mm beads, 4 4-mm beads)
Round coral beads (8 4-mm beads, 1 7-mm bead)
44 1 x 2.4-mm metal rings (gold)
2 crimp beads
Spring clasp
Adjustable chain closure
Nylon thread (1 20-cm length, 1 70-cm length)
60cm nylon-coated wire

1

Make motif, beginning by stringing beads on center of 70cm nylon thread. Form an intersection in an onyx bead to close circle.

3-mm turquoise bead
Metal ring
★
3-mm onyx bead

2

Pass thread through rings, adding beads as you go. Tie threads together on perimeter of motif and finish off.

Metal ring
4-mm onyx bead
4-mm turquoise bead

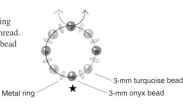

Add onyx and turquoise beads on perimeter of motif.

3

Make center of motif, using 20cm thread. Tie threads together and finish off.

7-mm coral bead
★

4

Pass nylon-coated wire through a 4-mm onyx bead. String beads on each side of onyx bead to make necklace, working in mirror image. Add a crimp bead at each end of necklace. Attach clasp to one end and adjustable chain closure to other.

Crimp bead
Clasp
4-mm coral bead
Metal rings
3 2-mm onyx beads
3-mm turquoise bead
Adjustable chain closure
A (4)
3-mm onyx bead
B (3)
A (3)
A (2)
B (1)
A (1)

Patterns

A 4-mm onyx bead
3 2-mm onyx beads

B Metal rings
3-mm turquoise bead
4-mm coral bead
3-mm onyx bead

Approximate size: 7 (US)
Motif diameter: 2cm

● Supplies (Ring)

Round onyx beads (28 2-mm beads, 17 3-mm beads, 4 4-mm beads)
Round turquoise beads (4 3-mm beads, 4 4-mm beads)
7-mm round coral bead
16 1 x 2.4-mm metal rings (gold)
Nylon thread (1 20-cm length, 2 70-cm lengths)

Make motif, referring to Steps 1-3 of instructions for necklace.
With 70cm nylon thread, pick up a 4-mm onyx bead on motif and weave band. Tie threads together and finish off.

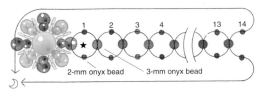

★
2-mm onyx bead
3-mm onyx bead

BALL NECKLACE & EARRINGS

Finished length (necklace): 71cm

● Supplies (Necklace)

Round green agate beads
(6 6-mm beads, 6 8-mm beads, 5 10-mm beads)
16 6-mm round coral beads
6-mm round freshwater pearl beads (16 white, 16 blue-gray)
16 5-mm round designer silver beads
82 2-mm round metal beads (gold)
32 1 x 2.4-mm metal rings (gold)
16 2 x 8-mm metal rings (gold)
2 1-cm lengths 0.6mm (inner diameter) coil or French wire (gold)
2 crimp beads
Clasp
90cm nylon-coated wire

String beads on nylon-coated wire, following patterns A-C (see drawing).
Attach each half of clasp to coil or French wire. Secure with crimp beads.

Patterns

A

Silver bead
Coral bead
Metal bead
8-mm green agate bead
Freshwater pearl bead
1 x 2.4-mm metal ring
Freshwater pearl bead (white)
2 x 8-mm metal ring

(Enlargement)

2 x 8-mm metal ring

Coral bead

B

6-mm green agate bead

Note: Except for the green agate beads, placement of beads in A-C is the same.

C

10-mm green agate bead

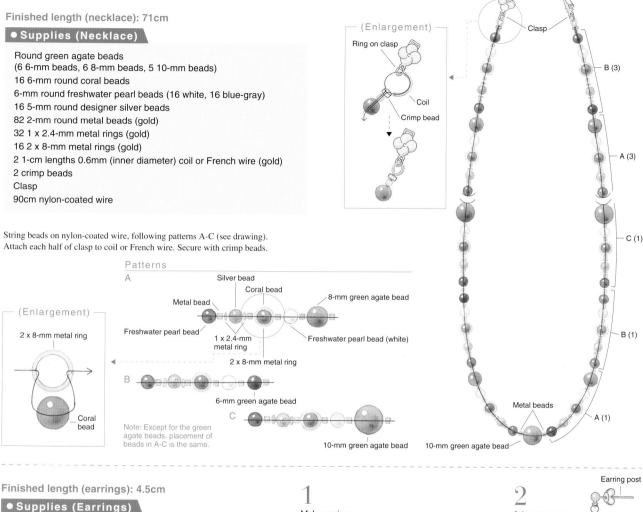

Clasp

(Enlargement)
Ring on clasp
Coil
Crimp bead

B (3)

A (3)

C (1)

B (1)

A (1)

Metal beads

10-mm green agate bead

Finished length (earrings): 4.5cm

● Supplies (Earrings)

2 8-mm round green agate beads
2 6-mm round coral beads
6-mm round freshwater pearl beads (2 white, 2 blue-gray)
6 2 x 8-mm metal rings (gold)
2 2 x 10-mm metal rings (gold)
2 1-cm lengths 0.6mm (inner diameter) coil
   or French wire (gold)
6 2-cm eyepins
2 2-cm headpins
Earring posts

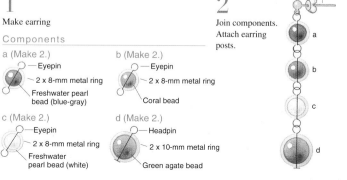

1
Make earring
Components

a (Make 2.)
Eyepin
2 x 8-mm metal ring
Freshwater pearl bead (blue-gray)

b (Make 2.)
Eyepin
2 x 8-mm metal ring
Coral bead

c (Make 2.)
Eyepin
2 x 8-mm metal ring
Freshwater pearl bead (white)

d (Make 2.)
Headpin
2 x 10-mm metal ring
Green agate bead

2
Join components.
Attach earring posts.

Earring post

a

b

c

d

11

RETRO-MODERN STYLE

We used matte gemstones in these designs to evoke days gone by. Tiny rose motifs and shell-shaped metal beads add touches of refinement.

Square Brooches

The eye-catching colors in these brooches are unified by black or brown beads. Smaller beads surround the gemstone beads and accentuate the square shape of the brooches.

Instructions: p. 14

Berry Necklace

Berry-shaped components dangle from the necklace, which features a large, central red bead. The slightly off-balance, asymmetrical design makes this piece even more striking.

Instructions: p. 15

SQUARE BROOCHES

Finished measurements: 3 x 3cm

● Supplies (Black brooch)

2 8-mm round green aventurine beads
2 8-mm round rutile quartz beads
4 6-mm round red agate beads
36 2-mm round onyx beads
20 2-mm 3-cut beads (gold: T CR712)
7-mm square cubic zirconia bead (black)
15-mm (diameter) perforated pin back
Nylon thread (2 30-cm lengths, 1 80-cm length)

Finished measurements: 3 x 3cm

● Supplies (Brown brooch)

2 8-mm round tiger's-eye beads
2 8-mm round freshwater pearl beads (gray)
4 6-mm round red aventurine beads
36 2-mm round gold sandstone beads
20 2-mm 3-cut beads (bronze: T CR221)
7-mm square cubic zirconia (yellow)
15-mm (diameter) perforated pin back
Nylon thread (2 30-cm lengths, 1 80-cm length)

1

String beads on center of nylon thread,
weaving figure eights as you go.

Green aventurine bead

4 onyx beads

Red agate bead

Rutile quartz bead

2 3-cut beads

2

Add onyx beads, working around perimeter
of brooch. Tie threads together and finish off.

Onyx bead

3

Make center of brooch,
using 30cm nylon thread.
Tie threads together and
finish off.

3-cut beads

Cubic zirconia

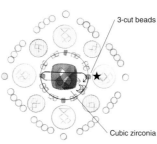

4

Using 30cm nylon thread,
attach motif to pin back
(see instructions on p. 77).

Perforated pin back

Attach motif here.

Cut tabs in half

Bottom of perforated
pin back

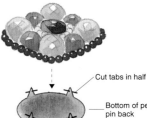

BERRY NECKLACE

Finished length: 42cm

● Supplies

5 6-mm round red agate beads
7 5-mm round turquoise beads
5 4-mm round gold sandstone beads
3 5-mm round labradorite beads
Round onyx beads (168 2-mm beads, 15 4-mm beads)
13 x 18-mm teardrop glass bead (red)
10 2.2-mm round silver beads
5 round 5-mm designer silver beads
28 thin 5-cm headpins with ball ends
2 crimp beads
7 3-mm jump rings
Spring clasp
Adjustable chain closure
30cm Artistic Wire
60cm nylon-coated wire

1

Make necklace components.

Components

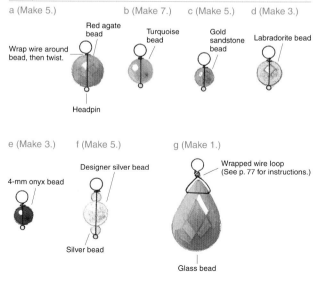

a (Make 5.)

Wrap wire around
bead, then twist.

Red agate
bead

Headpin

b (Make 7.)

Turquoise
bead

c (Make 5.)

Gold
sandstone
bead

d (Make 3.)

Labradorite bead

e (Make 3.)

4-mm onyx bead

f (Make 5.)

Designer silver bead

Silver bead

g (Make 1.)

Wrapped wire loop
(See p. 77 for instructions.)

Glass bead

2

String jump rings joining components and beads on nylon-coated wire to make
necklace. Add a crimp bead at each end of necklace.
Attach clasp to one end and adjustable chain closure to other.

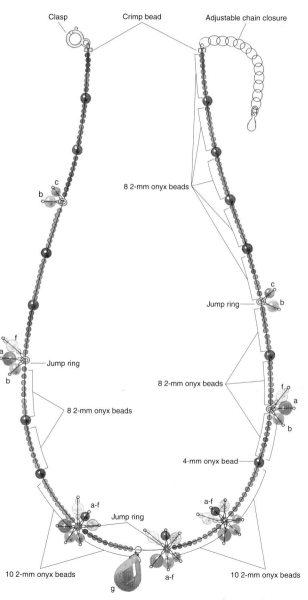

Clasp

Crimp bead

Adjustable chain closure

8 2-mm onyx beads

Jump ring

Jump ring

8 2-mm onyx beads

8 2-mm onyx beads

4-mm onyx bead

a-f

a-f

Jump ring

10 2-mm onyx beads

a-f

10 2-mm onyx beads

g

CLASSIC STYLE

Pearl jewelry has been a symbol of luxury and elegance throughout the ages. We made one motif in the shape of a ribbon, and combined pearl and coral beads for the other. Silver beads make an appearance in all three pieces.

Coral Ring

The diamond-shaped motif, with its three-dimensional look, is studded with bright coral beads. Try wearing this ring with the ribbon necklace!

Instructions: p. 19

Ribbon Necklace & Ring

The novel design of this necklace places the ribbon motif at the side. The combination of freshwater pearl and silver beads, and the rhinestone at the center of the ribbon give this classic a fresh, new image.

Instructions: pp. 18-19

RIBBON NECKLACE & RING

Finished length (necklace): 36cm
Motif measurements: 1.8 x 3cm

● Supplies (Necklace)

Round white freshwater pearl beads (16 3-mm beads, 12 4-mm
  beads, 74 5-mm beads)
64 2-mm seed beads (silver: M181)
3 x 10-mm rhinestone in four-pronged mounting (crystal)
2 crimp beads
Clasp set
Nylon thread (2 20-cm lengths, 1 80-cm length)
60cm nylon-coated wire

1

Make motif,
stringing beads on
80cm nylon thread.

2 seed beads
3-mm freshwater pearl bead
4-mm freshwater pearl bead
Seed bead
3-mm freshwater pearl bead
Rhinestone
4-mm freshwater pearl bead
★

2

Form an intersection in 3 seed beads.
Set both ends of thread aside.

3 seed beads
2 seed beads
4-mm freshwater pearl bead
Set both ends of thread aside.
3-mm freshwater pearl bead

String 2 seed beads and
4-mm freshwater pearl
bead, then form an
intersection in a 3-mm
freshwater pearl bead.

3

Weave right side of motif,
using 20cm nylon thread.
Tie threads together and
finish off.

Seed bead
4-mm freshwater pearl bead
★

4

With threads set aside in
Step 2, work around
perimeter of motif while
stringing seed beads.
Tie threads together and
finish off.

Seed beads
Seed beads
5 seed beads

5

Make back of motif, using 20cm nylon thread. Pass nylon-coated wire through
5-mm freshwater pearl bead on back of motif, and make necklace.
Add a crimp bead at each end of necklace. Attach clasp.

5-mm freshwater pearl bead
3-mm freshwater pearl bead
★
Back of motif
Clasp
Crimp beads
43 5-mm freshwater pearl beads
30 5-mm freshwater pearl beads
5-mm pearl bead on back of motif

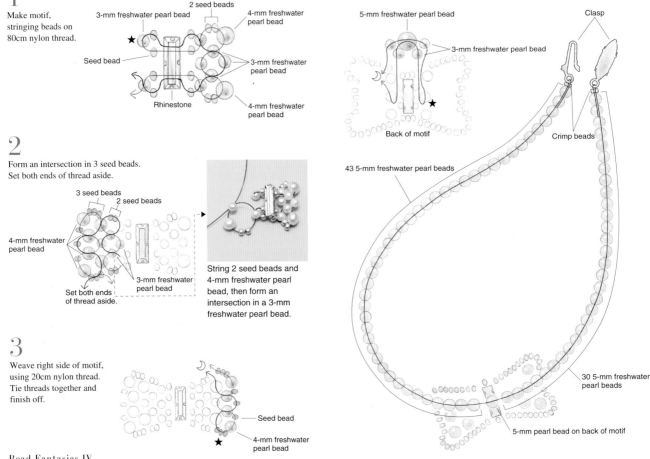
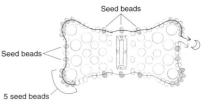

Approximate size: 7 (US)
Motif diameter: 1.5 x 3cm

● Supplies (Ring)

Round white freshwater pearl beads (35 3-mm beads, 14 4-mm beads)
64 2-mm seed beads (silver: M181)
3 x 10-mm rhinestone in 4-pronged mounting (crystal)
Nylon thread (1 20-cm length, 1 50-cm length, 1 80-cm length)

Make motif, referring to Steps 1-4 of instructions for necklace. Pick up seed beads on motif with 50cm thread, and weave band. Tie threads together and finish off.

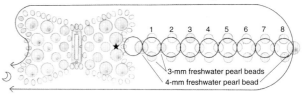

3-mm freshwater pearl beads
4-mm freshwater pearl bead

Classic Style
CORAL RING

Approximate size: 6 (US)
Motif diameter: 1.5 x 2.5cm

● Supplies

Round white freshwater pearl beads (23 3-mm beads, 4 4-mm beads)
Round coral beads (8 3-mm beads, 4 4-mm beads)
79 2-mm seed beads (silver: M181)
Nylon thread (1 60-cm length, 1 80-cm length)

1

Make motif, using
80cm nylon thread.

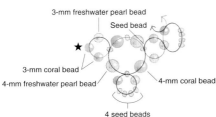

3-mm freshwater pearl bead
Seed bead
3-mm coral bead
4-mm freshwater pearl bead
4-mm coral bead
4 seed beads

2

Add more beads,
forming intersections
in 4 seed beads.

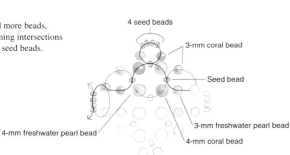

4 seed beads
3-mm coral bead
Seed bead
4-mm freshwater pearl bead
3-mm freshwater pearl bead
4-mm coral bead

3

Add seed beads
around perimeter of
motif. Tie threads
together and finish off.

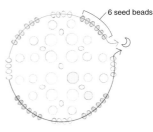

6 seed beads

4

Pick up seed beads on motif with
60cm nylon thread, and weave band.
Tie threads together and finish off.

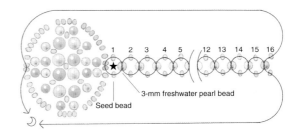

3-mm freshwater pearl bead
Seed bead

Gothic Cross Necklace

This design begins with a spacer bar, onto which freshwater pearl beads are woven to form a cross. Garnet beads are added for lovely accents.

Instructions: p. 22

GOTHIC STYLE

For our Gothic-style pieces, we selected the cross, of course, and a key charm (said to bring good luck). The resulting impression has just the right amount of mysticism. The freshwater pearl beads, in pale hues, and lengths of chain keep these pieces from becoming too heavy.

Key Charm Necklace & Earrings

The key charms represent home and hearth, since keys are believed to protect our residences. They also add movement to these pieces, with their acorn-shaped motifs.

Instructions: p. 23

GOTHIC CROSS NECKLACE

Finished length (necklace): 56cm
Motif diameter: 2.5 x 3.5cm

● Supplies

184 3-mm round freshwater pearl beads (gray)
10 4-mm round garnet beads
56 2-mm seed beads (black: M451)
3 17-mm 3-hole spacer bars
17-mm 5-hole spacer bar
2 crimp beads
Spring clasp
Adjustable chain closure
Nylon thread (3 40-cm lengths, 1 60-cm length)
80cm nylon-coated wire

1

String beads so as to enclose spacer bars, using 60cm nylon thread.

Freshwater pearl bead
5-hole spacer bar — Seed beads
★

Form a cross by weaving freshwater pearl beads onto 5-hole spacer bars.

2

Form a circle from seed beads. Add freshwater pearl beads. Tie threads together and finish off. Make bottom of cross, using 40cm nylon thread. Tie threads together and finish off.

8 seed beads

Freshwater pearl beads

Freshwater pearl beads

3

Make sides of cross, using 40cm nylon thread and working in mirror image. Tie threads together and finish off.

Freshwater pearl bead
Seed bead

String freshwater pearl and seed beads. Pass one end of thread back through seed beads, freshwater pearl beads and holes in spacer bar.

4

Pass nylon-coated wire through circle of seed beads at top of cross made in Step 2. String beads to make necklace. Add a crimp bead at each end of necklace. Attach clasp to one end and adjustable chain closure to other.

Clasp
Crimp beads
Adjustable chain closure
Seed bead
3 freshwater pearl beads
5
4
3
2
1

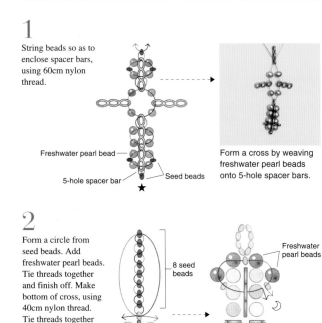

Pattern

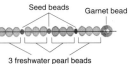

Seed beads   Garnet bead

3 freshwater pearl beads

KEY CHARM NECKLACE & EARRINGS

Finished length (necklace): 60cm

● Supplies (Necklace)

- 5 10-mm round green agate beads
- 75 2-mm round green sandstone beads
- 50 2-mm round red agate beads
- 35 2-mm round howlite beads
- 2 8-mm baroque freshwater pearl beads (white)
- 2 8-mm round Swarovski crystal beads (Dorado 2X)
- 10-mm round Swarovski crystal bead (jet)
- 11 x 16-mm teardrop Swarovski #6090 crystal bead (crystal aurora)
- 1 x 3-cm key charm (gold)
- 8 5-cm thick headpins with ball ends (gold)
- 2 5-cm thin headpins with ball ends (gold)
- 14 4-mm jump rings
- 58cm designer chain
- Spring clasp
- Adjustable chain closure
- 5 50-cm lengths nylon thread

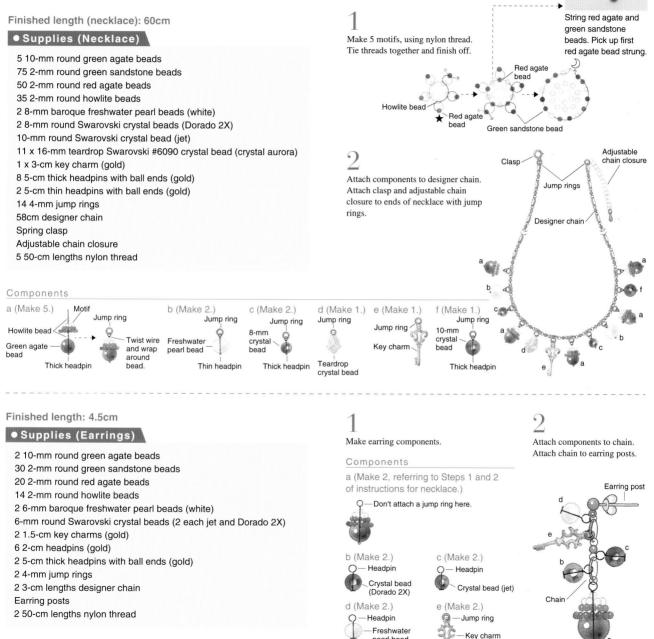

1 Make 5 motifs, using nylon thread. Tie threads together and finish off.

String red agate and green sandstone beads. Pick up first red agate bead strung.

Red agate bead
Howlite bead
★ Red agate bead
Green sandstone bead

2 Attach components to designer chain. Attach clasp and adjustable chain closure to ends of necklace with jump rings.

Clasp
Jump rings
Adjustable chain closure
Designer chain

Components

a (Make 5.)
Motif
Jump ring
Howlite bead
Green agate bead
Twist wire and wrap around bead.
Thick headpin

b (Make 2.)
Jump ring
Freshwater pearl bead
Thin headpin

c (Make 2.)
Jump ring
8-mm crystal bead
Thick headpin

d (Make 1.)
Jump ring
Teardrop crystal bead

e (Make 1.)
Jump ring
Key charm

f (Make 1.)
Jump ring
10-mm crystal bead
Thick headpin

Finished length: 4.5cm

● Supplies (Earrings)

- 2 10-mm round green agate beads
- 30 2-mm round green sandstone beads
- 20 2-mm round red agate beads
- 14 2-mm round howlite beads
- 2 6-mm baroque freshwater pearl beads (white)
- 6-mm round Swarovski crystal beads (2 each jet and Dorado 2X)
- 2 1.5-cm key charms (gold)
- 6 2-cm headpins (gold)
- 2 5-cm thick headpins with ball ends (gold)
- 2 4-mm jump rings
- 2 3-cm lengths designer chain
- Earring posts
- 2 50-cm lengths nylon thread

1 Make earring components.

Components

a (Make 2, referring to Steps 1 and 2 of instructions for necklace.)
Don't attach a jump ring here.

b (Make 2.)
Headpin
Crystal bead (Dorado 2X)

c (Make 2.)
Headpin
Crystal bead (jet)

d (Make 2.)
Headpin
Freshwater pearl bead

e (Make 2.)
Jump ring
Key charm

2 Attach components to chain. Attach chain to earring posts.

Earring post
d
e
c
b
Chain
a

OPULENT STYLE

Jewelry made with large gemstone beads simply exudes brilliance and luxury, and small-bead decorations add elegance to the motifs.

Royal Necklace & Ring

The elegant, substantial motifs on these pieces resemble crowns. The strands of tiny seed beads frame the round gemstone beads gracefully. We suggest wearing the turquoise pieces in the spring and summer, and the red agate pieces when cold weather arrives.

Instructions: pp. 26-27

ROYAL NECKLACE & RING

Finished length (necklace): 51cm **Motif diameter: 3cm**	**Finished length (necklace): 51cm** **Motif diameter: 3cm**

● Supplies (Blue necklace)	● Supplies (Red necklace)
12 6-mm round turquoise beads	12 6-mm round red agate beads
8 6-mm round moonstone beads	8 6-mm round moonstone beads
Round white freshwater pearl beads (8 4.5-mm beads, 4 6-mm beads)	Round white freshwater pearl beads (8 4.5-mm beads, 4 6-mm beads)
4 6-mm round Swarovski crystal beads (white opal)	4 6-mm round Swarovski crystal beads (white opal)
4 4-mm round metal beads (gold)	4 4-mm round metal beads (gold)
8 2-mm round metal beads (gold)	8 2-mm round metal beads (gold)
1.5-mm seed beads (80 gold-coated: M193, 80 blue: M347)	1.5-mm seed beads (80 gold-coated: M193, 80 red: M335)
8 2-mm seed beads (gold: M182)	8 2-mm seed beads (gold: M182)
730 1-mm 2-cut beads (bronze: M457)	730 1-mm 2-cut beads (bronze: M457)
8-mm rhinestone in 4-pronged mounting (milky white)	8-mm rhinestone in 4-pronged mounting (milky white)
Spring clasp	Spring clasp
Adjustable chain closure	Adjustable chain closure
Nylon thread (1 30-cm length, 1 100-cm length)	Nylon thread (1 30-cm length, 1 100-cm length)
2 80-cm lengths nylon-coated wire	2 80-cm lengths nylon-coated wire

1

Make motif, using 100cm nylon thread. Weave beads, forming intersections as you go. After working one round, set one end of thread aside.

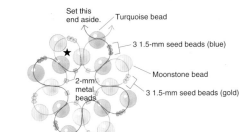

Set this end aside.
Turquoise bead
3 1.5-mm seed beads (blue)
Moonstone bead
3 1.5-mm seed beads (gold)
2-mm metal beads

2

String 1.5-mm seed beads on thread, 9 at a time. Set thread aside after working one round.

9 1.5-mm seed beads (gold)
9 1.5-mm seed beads (blue)
Set this end aside.

String 9 1.5-mm seed beads and a turquoise bead. Bring thread out at top of motif.

3

Working around perimeter of motif, string 8 1.5-mm seed beads at a time on thread set aside in Step 1.

8 1.5-mm seed beads (blue)
8 1.5-mm seed beads (gold)

4

Working around perimeter of motif, string freshwater pearl beads on both ends of thread. Tie threads together and finish off.

4.5-mm freshwater pearl beads

5

Make center of motif, using 30cm thread. Place rhinestone on top of motif to attach.

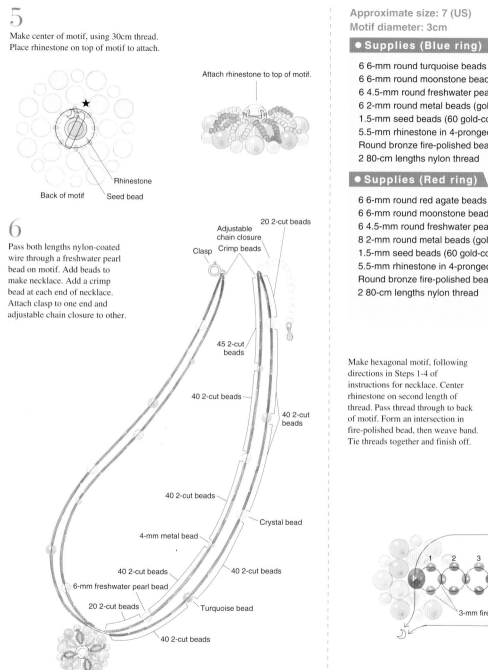

Back of motif

Rhinestone

Seed bead

Attach rhinestone to top of motif.

6

Pass both lengths nylon-coated wire through a freshwater pearl bead on motif. Add beads to make necklace. Add a crimp bead at each end of necklace. Attach clasp to one end and adjustable chain closure to other.

20 2-cut beads

Adjustable chain closure

Clasp

Crimp beads

45 2-cut beads

40 2-cut beads

40 2-cut beads

40 2-cut beads

Crystal bead

4-mm metal bead

40 2-cut beads

40 2-cut beads

6-mm freshwater pearl bead

20 2-cut beads

Turquoise bead

40 2-cut beads

Approximate size: 7 (US)
Motif diameter: 3cm

● Supplies (Blue ring)

6 6-mm round turquoise beads
6 6-mm round moonstone beads
6 4.5-mm round freshwater pearl beads (white)
6 2-mm round metal beads (gold)
1.5-mm seed beads (60 gold-coated: M193, 60 blue: M347)
5.5-mm rhinestone in 4-pronged mounting (milky white)
Round bronze fire-polished beads (41 3-mm beads, 1 4-mm bead)
2 80-cm lengths nylon thread

● Supplies (Red ring)

6 6-mm round red agate beads
6 6-mm round moonstone beads
6 4.5-mm round freshwater pearl beads (white)
8 2-mm round metal beads (gold)
1.5-mm seed beads (60 gold-coated: M193, 60 red: M335)
5.5-mm rhinestone in 4-pronged mounting (milky white)
Round bronze fire-polished beads (41 3-mm beads, 1 4-mm bead)
2 80-cm lengths nylon thread

Make hexagonal motif, following directions in Steps 1-4 of instructions for necklace. Center rhinestone on second length of thread. Pass thread through to back of motif. Form an intersection in fire-polished bead, then weave band. Tie threads together and finish off.

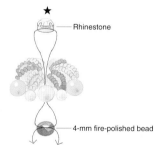

Rhinestone

4-mm fire-polished bead

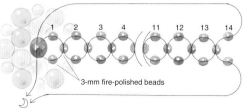

3-mm fire-polished beads

Magnificent Style

This brooch is as sophisticated as it is gorgeous. It is also very versatile, and pairs beautifully with handbags and hats, as well as apparel.

Autumn Flower Brooch

We made our flower from red jasper beads to set an autumn mood. The petals are crowned with lovely coral beads and delineated with tiny seed beads. Viewed from any angle, this brooch is dazzling.

Instructions: p. 29

Magnificent Style
AUTUMN FLOWER BROOCH

Diameter: 5cm

● Supplies

10 7.5 x 16-mm oval red jasper beads
10 2-mm round coral beads
10 3.5-mm round freshwater pearl beads (beige)
10 6-mm round fire-polished beads (iridescent green)
10-mm round cat's-eye bead (brown)
30 2-mm 3-cut beads (bronze: T CR221)
200 1.5-mm seed beads (bronze: T 221)
25-mm (diameter) perforated brooch back
Nylon-coated wire (1 30-cm length, 1 100-cm length)

1

Make motif, using
100cm nylon thread.

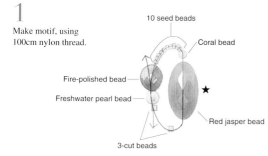

- 10 seed beads
- Coral bead
- Fire-polished bead
- Freshwater pearl bead
- ★
- Red jasper bead
- 3-cut beads

2

After working around motif once, form
intersections in 3-cut beads at center of motif.
Set one end of thread aside.

Set this end aside.

String 10 seed beads on
one end of thread, and
3-cut beads on the other.
Form intersections in coral
and red jasper beads.

3

Pass other end of thread through
3-cut beads at center of motif.
Tie to thread end set aside
earlier and finish off.

4

Attach motif to perforated brooch back,
using 30cm thread. Attach cat's-eye bead
to center. Join halves of brooch back
(see p. 77 for instructions).

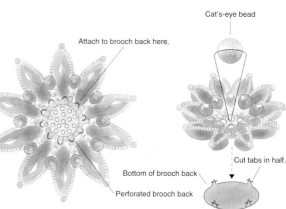

Cat's-eye bead

Attach to brooch back here.

Cut tabs in half.

Bottom of brooch back

Perforated brooch back

Hessonite Garnet
Necklace & Ring

This design emphasizes the transparency of the beautiful Hessonite garnet beads. The large mother-of-pearl beads at the center of the motifs and on the necklace exude refinement.

Instructions: pp. 32-33

BRITISH STYLE

We designed the pieces in this section to complement traditional British apparel, such as tweed jackets. Beads in warm colors help retain a feminine feel.

Tiger's-Eye Brooch

This is a simple design, made by arranging two different types of teardrop beads in a circle, and adding accent beads.

Instructions: p. 33

HESSONITE GARNET NECKLACE & RING

Finished length (necklace): 41cm
Motif diameter: 2cm

● Supplies (Necklace)

34 3.5-mm button hessonite garnet beads
8 teardrop hessonite garnet beads from 5mm-10mm in length
5 6-mm round mother-of-pearl beads (white)
19 2-mm seed beads (silver: M 181)
252 1.5-mm 3-cut beads (brown: T CRS421)
12 5-mm flat designer silver beads
2 crimp beads
Spring clasp
Adjustable chain closure
Nylon thread (1 20-cm length, 1 80-cm length)
80cm nylon-coated wire

1

Make motif, using
80cm nylon thread.

Silver bead

★

Teardrop hessonite garnet bead

2

Weave foundation with seed
beads, picking up silver beads as
you go along. Make one round of
center of motif. Tie threads
together and finish off.

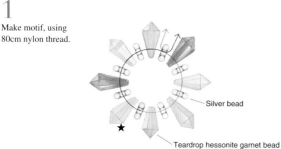

Form an intersection in a
seed bead. Don't pass thread
through hessonite garnet
bead this time.

Seed beads

3

Make center of motif, using
20cm thread. Tie threads
together and finish off.
Note: If center seems unstable,
secure it by applying epoxy to
the base of the hessonite garnet
and silver beads.

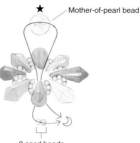

★   Mother-of-pearl bead

2 seed beads

4

String a seed bead on center of nylon-
coated wire. Pass both ends through a
seed bead on motif.

★

Seed bead

5

String beads on wire, working left
and right sides in mirror image. Add
a crimp bead at each end of necklace.
Attach clasp to one end and
adjustable chain closure to other.

Patterns

A

Mother-of-pearl bead

B   7 3-cut beads

Button hessonite
garnet beads

Silver bead

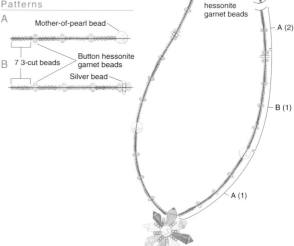

Clasp

Crimp beads

Adjustable
chain closure

7 3-cut
beads

B (2)

Button
hessonite
garnet beads

A (2)

B (1)

A (1)

Approximate size: 6 (US)
Motif diameter: 2cm

8 teardrop hessonite garnet beads varying 5mm-10mm in length
6-mm round mother-of-pearl bead (white)
84 2-mm seed beads (silver: M 181)
8 5-mm flat designer silver beads
Nylon thread (1 20-cm length, 2 80-cm lengths)

Make motif, referring to Steps 1-3 of instructions for necklace.
With 80cm nylon thread, pick up a seed bead on motif and weave band.
Tie threads together and finish off.

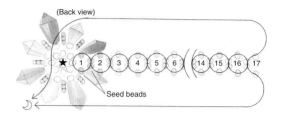

(Back view)

Seed beads

British Style
TIGER'S-EYE BROOCH

Diameter: 4cm

● Supplies

4 7 x 16-mm teardrop tiger's-eye beads
4 6.5 x 13-mm teardrop Swarovski crystal beads (Siam: #6000)
6-mm round rhinestone in 4-pronged mounting (milky white)
8 5-mm flat designer silver beads
16 3-mm seed beads (brown: T204)
2-cm (length) brooch back (silver)
Nylon thread (1 30-cm length, 1 80-cm length)

1
Make motif, using
80cm nylon thread.

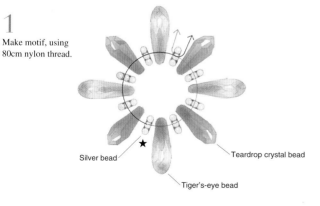

Silver bead

Tiger's-eye bead

Teardrop crystal bead

2
Make foundation round with
seed beads, picking up silver
beads as you go along. Pass
thread through seed beads.
Tie threads together and
finish off.

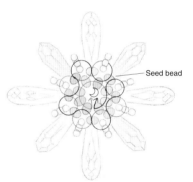

Seed bead

3
Attach rhinestone to brooch
back at center of motif, as
shown in drawing.
Tie threads together and
apply glue to knot for added
strength.

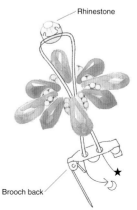

Rhinestone

Brooch back

33

British Style
Turquoise Necklace & Ring

The motif for this necklace and
ring are made in the same way as
the hessonite garnet motif on p. 30.
But the results look strikingly
different because turquoise gives
the appearance of greater weight
and volume. The subdued colors
of the accent beads make this a
sophisticated ensemble.

Instructions: p. 35

British Style
TURQUOISE
NECKLACE & RING

Finished length (necklace): 42cm
Motif diameter: 2cm

● Supplies (Necklace)

Turquoise beads (102 2-mm round beads, 8 4-mm round beads,
    6 5 x 7-mm teardrop beads)
9 5-mm round freshwater pearl beads (white)
8 4-mm bicone Swarovski crystal beads (jet)
38 2-mm seed beads (black: M401)
24 2-mm round metal beads (silver)
6 5-mm flat designer silver beads
2 crimp beads
Spring clasp
Adjustable chain closure
Nylon thread (1 20-cm length, 1 70-cm length)
70cm nylon-coated wire

1

Make motif, using
70cm nylon thread.

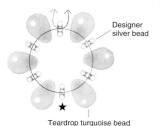

Teardrop turquoise bead

2

Make foundation with seed beads,
picking up designer silver beads as you
go along. Pass thread through beads at
center of motif. Tie threads together and
finish off.

Designer
silver bead

Seed bead

3

Make center of motif,
using 20cm nylon
thread. Tie threads
together and finish off.

★ Freshwater
pearl bead

Seed bead

4

String a seed bead on
center of nylon-coated
wire. Pass both ends of
wire through a seed bead in
motif, referring to drawing.

Seed
beads

5

String additional beads on wire to make necklace.
Add a crimp bead at each end of necklace. Attach
clasp to one end and adjustable chain closure to other.

Pattern

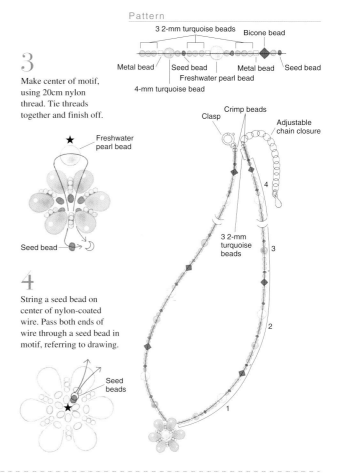

3 2-mm turquoise beads   Bicone bead

Metal bead   Seed bead   Metal bead   Seed bead
Freshwater pearl bead
4-mm turquoise bead

Clasp   Crimp beads

Adjustable
chain closure

3 2-mm
turquoise
beads

Size: 5 2 (US)
Motif diameter: 2cm

● Supplies (Ring)

Turquoise beads (50 2-mm round beads, 6 5 x 7-mm teardrop beads)
5-mm round freshwater pearl bead (white)
13 2-mm seed beads (black: M401)
6 5-mm flat designer silver beads
2 70-cm lengths nylon thread

Make motif, referring to Steps 1-2 of instructions for necklace. String freshwater
pearl bead on new length of thread, as in Step 3 of instructions for necklace, but
form an intersection in a seed bead instead of tying thread at back of motif. Use
same thread to make band. Tie threads together and finish off.

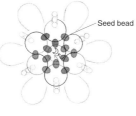

★ Freshwater pearl bead

Seed bead

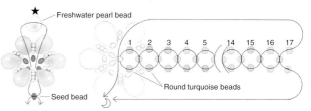

Round turquoise beads

BEADS & GEMSTONES

Here are descriptions of some of the beads used for the jewelry in this book.

1. 1-mm seed beads
2. Fire-polished beads: The surfaces of these faceted-glass beads are melted and then polished for added gloss.
3. Bicone crystal beads: Bicone describes two cones, base to base. We used Swarovski bicone crystal beads for the jewelry in this book.
4. 2-mm seed beads: Probably the most common size seed bead.
5. Triangle beads: As the name implies, these are shaped like a triangle; they shimmer in the light.

6. Round faceted beads: These add softness to a piece of jewelry; we used Swarovski beads for the jewelry in this book.
7.-9. Silver beads: These are available in a wide variety of shapes and styles.
10. 3-cut beads: These beads typically measure 2mm in diameter; the irregular cuts on their surfaces sparkle in the light.
11. 1-mm 3-cut beads
12. 3-mm seed beads
13. Cat's-eye beads: These have a streak at their centers that resembles a cta's eye.

14.-15. Button-shaped beads: Beads cut to look like flat buttons; 14. is made by Swarovski, and 15. are fire-polished.
16.-19. Metal beads and charms: These too come in an amazing range of styles; many are gold or silver-plated.
∗ Swarovski crystal beads
The Austrian firm Swarovski has been cutting crystals since 1895. Its precision machinery and beautiful, high-quality products have made the company world-famous. Swarovski beads enhance any piece of jewelry. Their product line is huge; bicones are perhaps the most popular shape.

Gemstones:
attributes and/ or magical properties

1. Peridot: Promises a bright future
2. Turquoise: Protects travelers
3. Apatite: Strengthens love
4. Green agate: Builds good relationships
5. Green aventurine: Creates opportunities
6. Amazonite: Brings love and hope
7. Green sandstone: Deep green stone with gold streaks
8. Amethyst: Enhances attractiveness and calms the nerves
9. Tanzanite: Reduces stress
10. Moonstone: Radiates light like the moon
11. Blue lace agate: Relaxes the mind

12. Freshwater pearl: Pearl cultivated in fresh water
13. Howlite: Alleviates sadness
14. Smoky quartz: Dispels fatigue
15. Labradorite: Drives away negative thoughts
16. Mother of pearl: Interior shell of an oyster; promotes happy marriages
17. Citirine: Improves financial and professional fortune
18. Rutile quartz: Cures fatigue
19. Jade: Found in a wide variety of hues
20. Carnelian: Ensures victory
21. Red aventurine: Calms the spirit
22. Coral: Slows aging

23. Pink opal: Gives hope
24. Gold sandstone: Brown gemstone with gold streaks
25. Sunstone: Provides opportunities
26. Rose quartz: Boosts romantic fortunes
27. Garnet: Increases vitality
28. Ruby: Symbol of passionate love
29. Onyx: Keeps trouble away
30. Red agate: Brings its wearer victory
31. Tiger's-eye: Boosts financial fortunes
32. Amber: Brings financial good fortune
33. Hessonite garnet: Symbolizes chastity and truth
34. Blue sandstone: Dark blue stone with gold streaks

Part 2
JEWELRY-
DESIGN
KEYWORDS

Besides weaving technique and color
arrangement, there are other ways to
add originality to an article of jewelry.
On the following pages, we will
present some keywords that stand for
innovative design ideas.

CUBIC ZIRCONIA

These sparkling, manmade gems refract almost as much light as diamonds.
They combine beautifully with gemstones and Swarovski beads.

Sparkling Flower Necklace & Ring

The flower motif features a light-brown cubic zirconia and citrine beads, for an understated look. The layered petals sparkle wonderfully in the light.

Instructions: p. 40

Luminous Ring

The diamond-shaped cubic zirconia has a bold presence.
The luscious grays and purples spell elegance.

Instructions: p. 41

Keyword 1: Cubic Zirconia

SPARKLING FLOWER NECKLACE & RING

Finished length (necklace): 40cm
Motif diameter: 2cm

● Supplies (Necklace)

6 5 x 7.5-mm teardrop cubic zirconia beads (light brown)
Citrine beads (8 4-mm button beads, 6 6.5 x 6-mm teardrop beads)
121 3-mm round freshwater pearl beads (white)
60 3-cut beads (gold: T CR712)
2 crimp beads
3-mm jump ring (gold)
13-mm (diameter) perforated necklace finding (gold)
Spring clasp
Adjustable chain closure
Nylon thread (1 40-cm length, 1 80-cm length)
60cm nylon-coated wire

1

Make motif, using
80cm nylon thread.

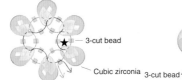

3-cut bead
Cubic zirconia   3-cut bead

2

Add 3-cut and citrine beads, picking up 3-cut
beads strung in Step 1. Tie threads
together and finish off.

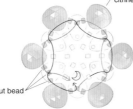

Teardrop citrine bead

3

Attach motif to perforated
finding, using 40cm nylon
thread. Sew freshwater pearl
bead onto finding at center of
motif. Join two halves of finding
(see p. 77 for instructions).

Freshwater pearl bead

Attach to finding here.

Bottom of finding ▼

Perforated finding

Cut tabs in half.

4

String beads on nylon-coated wire
so that left and right sides of
necklace are in mirror image. Add a
crimp bead at each end of necklace.
Attach clasp to one end and
adjustable chain closure to other.

Adjustable chain closure

Clasp

Crimp beads

3-cut beads

3 freshwater pearl beads

Jump ring

Pattern

3-cut beads   Button citrine beads

3 freshwater pearl beads

Approximate size: 6 2 (US)
Motif diameter: 2cm

● Supplies (Ring)

6 5 x 7.5-mm teardrop cubic zirconia beads (light brown)
6 6.5 x 6-mm teardrop citrine beads
21 3-mm round freshwater pearl beads (white)
74 3-cut beads (gold: T CR712)
Nylon thread (1 60-cm length, 1 80-cm length)

1

Make motif, referring to Steps 1-2 of
instructions for necklace. String a freshwater
pearl bead on center of 60cm thread; with
same thread, form an intersection in 2 3-cut
beads on back of motif.

2

Weave band. Tie threads together
and finish off.

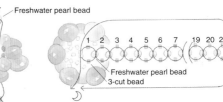

★ Freshwater pearl bead

2 3-cut beads

Freshwater pearl bead
3-cut bead

LUMINOUS RING

Approximate size: 7 (US)
Motif diameter: 2cm

● Supplies (Gray ring)

10 x 15-mm diamond-shaped cubic zirconia bead (light brown)
6 3-mm round freshwater pearl beads (blue-gray)
3-mm round Swarovski crystal beads (4 light Colorado satin, 4 crystal satin)
6 4-mm round Swarovski crystal beads (light Colorado satin)
6 4-mm bicone Swarovski crystal beads (crystal satin)
32 3-mm fire-polished beads (crystal CAL)
10 2-mm round silver beads
4 2-mm round labradorite beads
Nylon thread (1 60-cm length, 1 80-cm length)

● Supplies (Purple ring)

10 x 15-mm diamond-shaped cubic zirconia bead (lavender)
6 3-mm round freshwater pearl beads (white)
3-mm round Swarovski crystal beads (4 peridot satin, 4 violet)
6 4-mm round Swarovski crystal beads (peridot satin)
6 4-mm bicone Swarovski crystal beads (violet)
32 3-mm fire-polished beads (purple CAL)
10 2-mm round silver beads
4 2-mm round amethyst beads
Nylon thread (1 60-cm length, 1 80-cm length)

1

Make motif, using 80cm nylon thread.

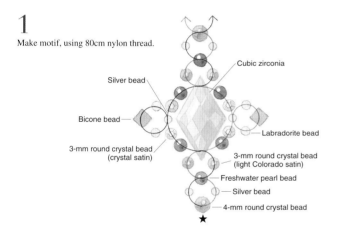

Cubic zirconia
Silver bead
Bicone bead
3-mm round crystal bead (crystal satin)
Labradorite bead
3-mm round crystal bead (light Colorado satin)
Freshwater pearl bead
Silver bead
4-mm round crystal bead

2

Add beads, picking up beads added to perimeter of motif in Step 1. Tie threads together and finish off.

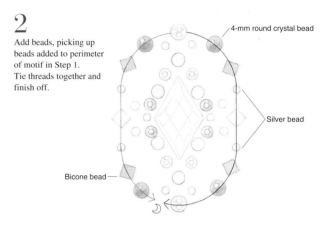

4-mm round crystal bead
Silver bead
Bicone bead

3

Pick up a bicone bead on motif with 60cm thread, and weave motif. Tie threads together and finish off.

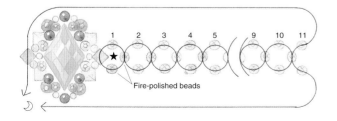

Fire-polished beads

About cubic zirconias

A colorless, transparent cubic zirconia looks just like a diamond. This manmade stone was first manufactured in Russia in the 1970s. Its sparkling beauty and reasonable price have created a demand for it as a component in jewelry. Besides the colorless version, cubic zirconias are now manufactured in several colors. Their light refraction properties are enhanced when combined with gemstones or Swarovski crystal beads.

Keyword 2
SETTINGS

Settings come in handy when you're working with gemstones or Swarovski crystals with no holes. They also add a touch of luxury. Once you set these stones, you can weave them as you would any other beads.

Marigold Brooch

This hexagonal brooch features six petals framed with blue sandstone beads. The gold mountings enhance the brilliance of the Swarovski crystal beads.

Instructions: p. 45

Dual-Cross Necklace

Here we set beads in four colors to make two intersecting crosses. To keep the mountings from touching each other, and thus giving the pieces a weighty look, we separated them with black and bronze beads.

Instructions: p. 44

DUAL-CROSS NECKLACES

Finished length: 45cm
Motif diameter: 3cm

● Supplies (Blue necklace)

5 x 10-mm oval flat-back Swarovski crystals (2 turquoise, 2 Pacific opal)
4 5 x 10-mm 4-pronged oval mountings (gold)
4 x 8-mm oval flat-back Swarovski crystals
(2 aquamarine satin, 2 white alabaster)
4 4 x 8-mm 4-pronged oval mountings (gold)
4-mm bicone Swarovski crystal beads
(4 turquoise, 6 Pacific opal, 4 aquamarine satin, 6 white alabaster)
10 3-mm round fire-polished beads (jet)
24 3-mm round glass beads (bronze)
2-mm seed beads (12 black: M401, 200 bronze: M457)
40 1.6-mm 3-cut beads (gold: T CRS712)
2 crimp beads
Spring clasp
Adjustable chain closure
80cm nylon thread
60cm nylon-coated wire

Finished length: 45cm
Motif diameter: 3cm

● Supplies (Purple necklace)

5 x 10-mm oval flat-back Swarovski crystals
(2 light smoke topaz, 2 amethyst)
4 5 x 10-mm 4-pronged oval mountings (gold)
4 x 8-mm oval flat-back Swarovski crystals (2 peridot satin, 2 rose satin)
4-mm bicone Swarovski crystal beads
(4 light smoke topaz, 6 amethyst, 4 peridot satin, 6 rose satin)
10 3-mm round fire-polished beads (jet)
24 3-mm round glass beads (bronze)
2-mm seed beads (12 black: M401, 200 bronze: M457)
40 1.6-mm 3-cut beads (gold: T CRS712)
2 crimp beads
Spring clasp
Adjustable chain closure
80cm nylon thread
60cm nylon-coated wire

1

Set crystals in mountings; string mounted crystals and other beads on nylon thread to form a circle. Pass thread through beads in circle twice.

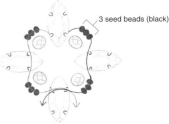

Crystal (Pacific opal)
Fire-polished bead
Crystal (turquoise)

2

Add black seed beads. Pass thread through holes in mounted crystals strung in Step 1.

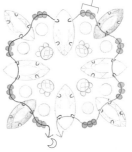

3 seed beads (black)

3

Pass thread through and form intersections in holes in mounted crystals first strung nearest perimeter. Add more mounted crystals.

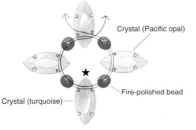

Mounted crystal (aquamarine satin)
Mounted crystal (white alabaster)
Round glass beads

4

Add bronze seed beads, passing thread through holes in mounted crystals strung in Step 3. Tie threads and finish off.

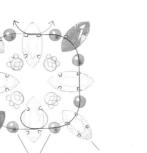

3 seed beads (bronze)

5

Pass nylon-coated wire through a mounted aquamarine satin crystal on motif. String beads on wire to make necklace (left and right sides should be in mirror image). Add a crimp bead at each end of necklace. Attach clasp to one end and adjustable chain closure to other.

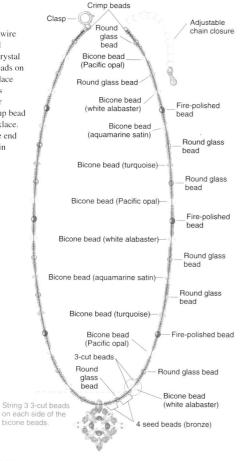

Crimp beads
Clasp
Round glass bead
Adjustable chain closure
Bicone bead (Pacific opal)
Round glass bead
Bicone bead (white alabaster)
Fire-polished bead
Bicone bead (aquamarine satin)
Round glass bead
Bicone bead (turquoise)
Round glass bead
Bicone bead (Pacific opal)
Fire-polished bead
Bicone bead (white alabaster)
Round glass bead
Bicone bead (aquamarine satin)
Round glass bead
Bicone bead (turquoise)
Round glass bead
Bicone bead (Pacific opal)
Fire-polished bead
3-cut beads
Round glass bead
Round glass bead
Bicone bead (white alabaster)
4 seed beads (bronze)

String 3 3-cut beads on each side of the bicone beads.

About mountings

Place the stones (or crystals) in the mountings. Use pliers to bend the prongs down, but be careful not to damage stones.

Setting the stone

Place stone in mounting.

↓

Bend prongs on mounting down toward the stone.

→

Crystal set in mounting

MARIGOLD BROOCH

Finished diameter: 2.5cm

● Supplies

3 5 x 10-mm oval flat-back Swarovski crystals (padparadscha)
3 5 x 10-mm 4-pronged oval mountings (gold)
3 4 x 8-mm oval flat-back Swarovski crystals (topaz)
3 4 x 8-mm 4-pronged oval mountings (gold)
Round blue sandstone beads (21 2-mm beads, 6 4-mm beads)
12 2-mm 3-cut beads (black: T CR81)
5-mm round freshwater pearl bead (white)
15-mm (diameter) perforated brooch back (gold)
Nylon thread (1 30-cm length, 1 80-cm length)

1

Set crystals in mountings. Pass 80cm nylon thread through mounted crystals and beads twice.

3-cut beads
Large mounted crystal
Small mounted crystal

2

Add blue sandstone beads, passing thread through mounted crystals near perimeter of motif.

4-mm blue sandstone bead

3

Add 2-mm sandstone beads, working around perimeter of motif. Tie threads together and finish off.

4 2-mm blue sandstone beads

3 2-mm blue sandstone beads

4

Attach motif to brooch back, using 30cm thread. Add a freshwater pearl bead at center of motif. Join halves of brooch back (see p. 77 for instructions).

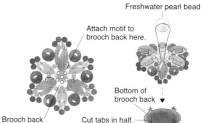

Freshwater pearl bead
Attach motif to brooch back here.
Brooch back
Bottom of brooch back
Cut tabs in half.

45

Keyword 3
FRINGE

Long, abundant strands of fringe make a necklace resplendent
and regal. In choosing the beads and colors for these pieces,
we aimed for a perfect balance.

Pink Jadeite Fringe Necklace

Teardrop pink jadeite beads and round blue and green
beads grace the strands of fringe on this breathtakingly
beautiful necklace, and add vitality.

Instructions: p. 48

Amazonite Fringe Necklace

The fringe on this festive necklace features oval amazonite beads.
We kept it short because we wanted a light, airy necklace.
The ruby beads at the top of the fringe have a richly elegant effect.

Instructions: p. 47

AMAZONITE FRINGE NECKLACE

Finished length: 39cm

● Supplies

11 6.5 x 8-mm oval amazonite beads
9 6-mm round turquoise beads
21 3 x 4-mm button ruby beads
13 3 x 5-mm button fire-polished beads (bronze)
15 4-mm bicone Swarovski crystal beads (burgundy AB2X)
138 2-mm 3-cut beads (bronze: T CR221)
16 2-cm eyepins
5 2-cm headpins
2 crimp beads
Spring clasp
Adjustable chain closure
60cm nylon-coated wire

1

Make necklace components.

Components

a (Make 5.)　b (Make 5.)　c (Make 5.)　d (Make 3.)　e (Make 3.)

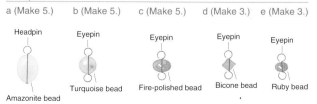

Headpin

Eyepin

Eyepin

Eyepin

Eyepin

Amazonite bead　Turquoise bead　Fire-polished bead　Bicone bead　Ruby bead

2

Join components. String beads on nylon-coated wire. Add a crimp bead at each end of necklace. Attach clasp to one end and adjustable chain closure to other.

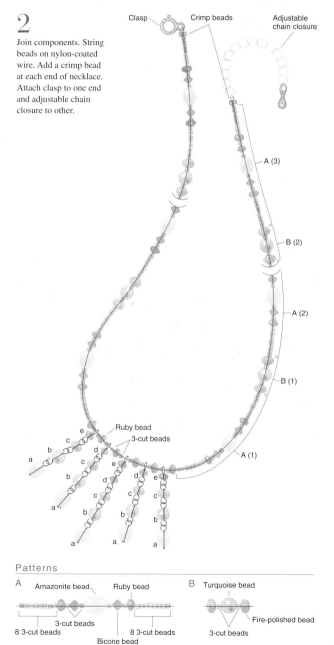

Clasp　Crimp beads　Adjustable chain closure

A (3)

B (2)

A (2)

B (1)

A (1)

e
c
b
a
c
b
a'
a
Ruby bead
3-cut beads
d
c
d
e
d
c
b
a
e
c
b
a

Patterns

A　Amazonite bead　Ruby bead

8 3-cut beads　3-cut beads　8 3-cut beads
Bicone bead

B　Turquoise bead

3-cut beads　Fire-polished bead

47

PINK JADEITE FRINGE NECKLACE

Finished length: 42cm

● Supplies

8 6-mm round pink jadeite beads
5 10 x 14-mm teardrop pink jadeite beads
13 4-mm round amazonite beads
13 4-mm round turquoise beads
11 4-mm round green agate beads
16 4-mm round Swarovski crystal beads (crystal aurora)
18 4-mm bicone Swarovski crystal beads (rose satin)
76 2-mm 3-cut beads (silver: M181)
9 2-cm eyepins
2 crimp beads
Spring clasp
Adjustable chain closure
5 20-cm lengths Artistic Wire
60cm nylon-coated wire

1

Make necklace components.

2

Join components. String beads on nylon-coated wire. Add a crimp bead at each end of necklace. Attach clasp to one end and adjustable chain closure to other.

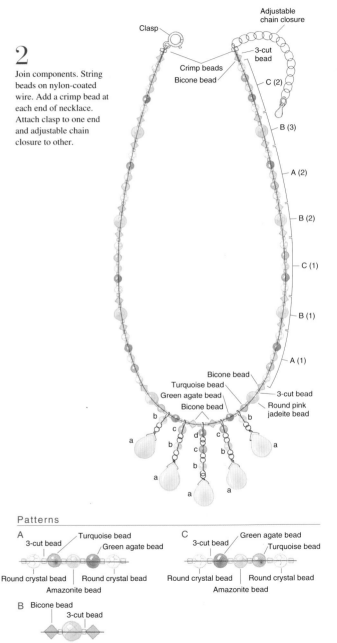

Clasp
Adjustable chain closure
Crimp beads
Bicone bead
3-cut bead
C (2)
B (3)
A (2)
B (2)
C (1)
B (1)
A (1)
Bicone bead
Turquoise bead
Green agate bead
Bicone bead
3-cut bead
Round pink jadeite bead

b c d c b b a a
b a

Components

a (Make 5.)

Wrap Artistic Wire around top of bead (see p. 77 for instructions).

Teardrop pink jadeite bead

b (Make 5.)

Eyepin

Amazonite bead

c (Make 3.)

Eyepin

Turquoise bead

d (Make 1.)

Eyepin

Green agate bead

Patterns

A
3-cut bead
Turquoise bead
Green agate bead
Round crystal bead
Round crystal bead
Amazonite bead

B
Bicone bead
3-cut bead
Round pink jadeite bead

C
3-cut bead
Green agate bead
Turquoise bead
Round crystal bead
Round crystal bead
Amazonite bead

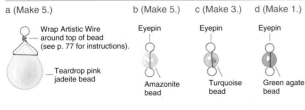

Keyword 4
WRAPS

Beads are wrapped around other beads in these delicate designs.
Our point was to enclose, not cover the larger,
diamond-shaped beads.

Wrap Necklaces & Rings

For these pieces, we surround large beads with a net of
smaller beads. At first glance, this necklace and ring
seem difficult to make, but once you've made the
netting that encloses the diamond-shaped beads, the
rest is easy.
Instructions: Mother-of-pearl set, p. 51; Green set, p. 52

MOTHER-OF-PEARL NECKLACE & RING

Finished length (necklace): 41cm
Motif size: 1.5 x 2cm

● Supplies (Necklace)

3 10 x 14-mm rectangular mother-of-pearl beads (brown)
6 6-mm round mother-of-pearl beads (brown)
20 4-mm round Swarovski crystal beads (crystal aurora)
272 2-mm round metal beads (silver)
2 crimp beads
Spring clasp
Adjustable chain closure
3 80-cm lengths nylon thread
60cm nylon-coated wire

1

Weave figure eights
with nylon thread.

Round
crystal bead

★ — Metal bead

2

Close the circle, then
make one layer of motif.

Round
crystal bead

5 metal beads

3

Make other layer of motif,
picking up round crystal
beads woven in Step 2.
When motif is nearly
completed, insert
rectangular mother-of-pearl
bead between layers so that
it is enclosed. Tie threads
together and finish off.
Make three of these.

5 metal
beads

Rectangular mother-
of-pearl bead

4

With nylon-coated wire,
pick up round crystal
beads on motif, and
string beads to make
necklace. Work left and
right sides in mirror
image. Add a crimp bead
at each end of necklace.
Attach clasp to one end
and adjustable chain
closure to other.

Adjustable chain closure

Clasp

Crimp beads

12 metal beads

Round
crystal bead

8 metal beads

3

2

1

8 metal beads

Pattern

Round crystal bead

Round mother-of-pearl bead

8 metal beads

Approximate size: 6 2 (US)
Motif size: 1.5 x 2cm

● Supplies (Ring)

10 x 14-mm rectangular mother-of-pearl bead (brown)
4 4-mm round Swarovski crystal beads (crystal aurora)
86 2-mm metal beads (silver)
Nylon thread (1 60-cm length, 1 80-cm length)

Make one motif, referring to Steps 1-3 of instructions for necklace. Pick up round
crystal and metal beads on motif and weave band. Tie threads together and finish off.

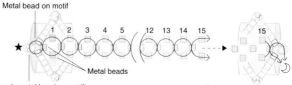

Metal bead on motif

★   1   2   3   4   5   12   13   14   15   15

Metal beads

Round crystal bead on motif

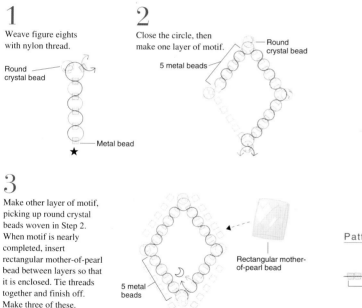

51

GREEN WRAP NECKLACE & RING

Finished length (necklace): 41cm
Motif size: 1.5 x 2cm

● Supplies (Necklace)

14 4-mm round garnet beads
140 2-mm gold sandstone beads
16 3-mm round Swarovski crystal beads (peridot satin)
12 x 16-mm oval designer bead (green)
136 1.5-mm seed beads (brown: M311)
2.5-cm headpin
2 crimp beads
Spring clasp
Adjustable chain closure
80cm nylon thread
60cm nylon-coated wire

1

Make motif by stringing beads on nylon thread.

3 gold sandstone beads
★ Bicone bead

2

Weave figure eights, picking up beads strung in Step 1 as you go along.

Gold sandstone beads
Seed beads
Garnet bead

3

Make perimeter of motif, picking up garnet beads woven in Step 2 and adding new beads. Add teardrop freshwater pearl beads onto foundation made in Step 2. When perimeter is nearly completed, insert designer bead into it so that it is enclosed. Tie threads together and finish off.

Seed beads
3 gold sandstone beads
Designer bead

4

Insert headpin into designer bead. Round end of headpin with pliers.

Headpin

5

Thread nylon-coated wire through circle at end of headpin. String beads on wire to make necklace, working in left-right mirror image. Add a crimp bead at each end of necklace. Attach clasp to one end and adjustable chain closure to other.

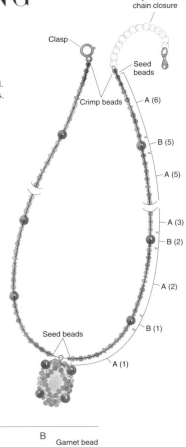

Adjustable chain closure
Clasp
Seed beads
Crimp beads
A (6)
B (5)
A (5)
A (3)
B (2)
A (2)
B (1)
A (1)
Seed beads

Patterns

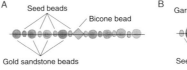

A
Seed beads
Bicone bead
Gold sandstone beads

B
Garnet bead
Seed beads

Approximate size: 7 (US)
Motif size: 1.5 x 2cm

● Supplies (Ring)

4 4-mm round garnet beads
88 2-mm round gold sandstone beads
4 3-mm bicone Swarovski crystal beads (peridot satin)
12 x 16-mm oval designer bead (green)
16 1.5-mm seed beads (brown: M311)
Nylon thread (1 60-cm length, 1 80-cm length)

Make motif, using 80cm nylon thread and referring to Steps 1-3 of instructions for necklace. With 60cm thread, pick up a gold sandstone bead on motif and weave band. Tie threads together and finish off.

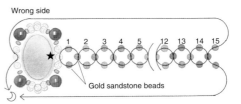

Wrong side
1 2 3 4 5 12 13 14 15
Gold sandstone beads

Wire Ring

Ball-end headpins frame a freshwater
pearl bead in this lovely ring.
A perfectly balanced single rhinestone
serves as the accent within the frame.
For best results, wrap the headpins
tightly around the wire.

Keyword 4: Wraps
WIRE RING

Approximate size: 6 2 (US)

● Supplies

10-12mm baroque freshwater pearl bead (white)
10 5-cm ball-end headpins (silver)
4-cm headpin with rhinestone end
70cm Artistic Wire

1

String a freshwater pearl bead
on center of Artistic Wire.
Shape wire with fingers,
referring to drawing.

Freshwater pearl bead

a   Shape wire   b
with fingers.

2

Wind component made in
Step 1 around a ring stick.

Ring stick

b

a

3

Push wire down into
the groove in ring stick
corresponding to your
ring size, and wind end
around freshwater
pearl bead. Wind other
end in same way. Cut
excess wire.

Groove in ring stick

a

Wind end of wire twice.

4

Remove ring from ring stick.
Wind headpins, including
headpin with rhinestone end,
tightly around wire near base
of freshwater pearl bead.

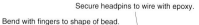

Secure headpins to wire with epoxy.

Bend with fingers to shape of bead.

Headpin with ball end

Headpin with rhinestone end

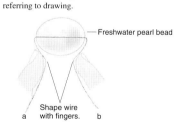

Wind 2-3
times.

Note: Headpins with
rhinestone ends will break
if you bend or pull on them
forcefully.

Keyword 5
COIL

You can simply string beads on these spirals of metal wire, but you can also cut and shape coil. Its luster lends an Oriental mood to jewelry.

Chignon Ring

Three lengths of coil decorate the round gemstone beads in this gorgeous ring. The color arrangement at the ring's center accentuates the lines formed by the coil.

Instructions: p. 56

Rose Quartz Necklace

For this necklace, we attached tiny coil circles and fringe adorned with pink jade beads to a large rose quartz bead. The pink jade bead fringe traces a fan-shaped curve.

Instructions: p. 57

Flower Loop Necklace

We joined five coil rings to make the flower motif, which we positioned between a freshwater pearl bead and a peridot bead for a bright accent.

Instructions: p. 56

Keyword 5: Coil
CHIGNON RING

Size: 6 2 (US)
Motif diameter: 2cm

● Supplies (Red ring)

- 6 6-mm round red agate beads
- 6 3-mm round carnelian beads
- 20 3-mm bicone Swarovski crystal beads (smoke topaz)
- 6 4-mm bicone Swarovski crystal beads (smoke topaz)
- 78 1.5-mm seed beads (gold: T22)
- 18 1-cm lengths 0.6mm (inner diameter) coil or French wire
- Nylon thread (1 60-cm length, 1 100-cm length)

About coil

Try using short lengths of coil on a necklace for a simple, elegant effect. We also used coil to attach a clasp to the necklace shown on p. 9.

Size: 6 2 (US)
Motif diameter: 2cm

● Supplies (Blue ring)

- 6 3-mm round amazonite beads
- 6 6-mm round amazonite beads
- 20 3-mm bicone Swarovski crystal beads (Pacific opal)
- 6 4-mm bicone Swarovski crystal beads (Pacific opal)
- 78 1.5-mm seed beads (gold: T22)
- 18 1-cm lengths 0.6mm (inner diameter) coil or French wire
- Nylon thread (1 60-cm length, 1 100-cm length)

Keyword 5: Coil
FLOWER LOOP NECKLACE

Finished length: 41cm
Motif diameter: 3cm

● Supplies

- 10 x 13-mm teardrop freshwater pearl bead (white)
- 84 3-mm round freshwater pearl beads (white)
- 8 4-mm button peridot beads
- 3 4 x 7-mm teardrop peridot beads
- 14 4-mm button garnet beads
- 26 2-mm round red aventurine beads
- 61 1.5-mm seed beads (gold: T22)
- 7 3-mm mirror-ball beads
- 5 1-cm lengths 0.6mm (inner diameter) coil or French wire
- 2 crimp beads
- 3 3-mm jump rings
- Spring clasp
- Adjustable chain closure
- 4 30-cm lengths Artistic Wire
- 60cm nylon-coated wire

3

String beads on nylon-coated wire, making left and right sides of necklace in mirror image. Add a crimp bead at each end of necklace. Attach clasp to one end and adjustable chain closure to other.

Patterns

A Button peridot bead
Seed bead
Round freshwater pearl bead

B Garnet bead
Red aventurine bead

C Mirror-ball bead
Seed bead
Round freshwater pearl bead

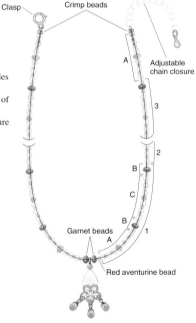

Clasp
Crimp beads
A
Adjustable chain closure
3
B
C
2
Garnet beads
A
B
1
Red aventurine bead

Mirror-ball bead
Teardrop freshwater pearl bead
Jump ring
Make a wrapped wire loop with Artistic Wire (see p. 77 for instructions).
Teardrop peridot bead

1

String lengths of coil and seed beads on Artistic Wire to make motif.

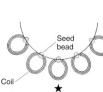

Seed bead
Coil
★

2

Pass both ends of wire used in Step 1 through teardrop freshwater pearl bead and mirror-ball bead. Then make a wrapped wire loop. Join peridot components to coil with jump rings.

1

Make motif, using 100cm nylon thread.

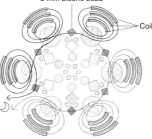

- 4-mm bicone bead
- Red agate bead
- Seed bead
- Carnelian bead

2

Pass thread through coil, adding 3-mm bicone beads as you go. Tie threads together and finish off.

- 3-mm bicone bead
- Coil

3

Pick up a bicone bead on motif with 60cm nylon thread. Weave band. Tie threads together and finish off.

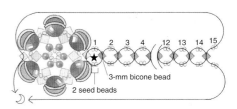

- 3-mm bicone bead
- 2 seed beads

Keyword 5: Coil

ROSE QUARTZ NECKLACE

Finished length: 41cm
Motif diameter: 3cm

● Supplies

12-mm round rose quartz bead
Pink jadeite beads (8 3.5 x 7-mm button beads, 14 4 x 5.5-mm oval beads, 5 5.5 x 7-mm teardrop beads)
6 3-mm button carnelian beads
21 3-mm bicone Swarovski crystal beads (light azore)
77 2-mm 3-cut beads (gold: T CR712)
155 1.5-mm seed beads (gold: T22)
3-mm round mirror-ball bead
5 1-cm lengths 0.6mm (inner diameter) coil or French wire
5 2-cm headpins
2 crimp beads
Spring clasp
Adjustable chain closure
40cm Artistic Wire
60cm nylon-coated wire

3

String beads on nylon-coated wire to make necklace, making left and right sides in mirror image. Add a crimp bead at each end of necklace. Attach clasp to one end and adjustable chain closure to other.

Patterns

A

- Bicone bead
- Oval pink jadeite bead
- 3-cut bead
- 5 seed beads
- 3-cut beads
- Button pink jadeite bead

B

- Carnelian bead
- Oval pink jadeite bead
- 5 seed beads
- 3-cut beads

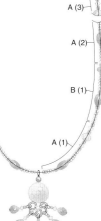

- Clasp
- Crimp beads
- Adjustable chain closure
- 5 seed beads
- A (4)
- B (3)
- A (3)
- A (2)
- B (1)
- A (1)

1

Make necklace components.

Components

a (Make 5.)

- Headpin
- 3-cut bead
- Bicone bead
- Teardrop pink jadeite bead

2

Make motif, referring to Steps 1-2 of instructions for Flower Loop Necklace, and substituting a rose quartz bead for the freshwater pearl bead. Join components to coil.

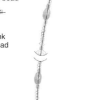

- Mirror-ball bead
- Coil
- Make a wrapped wire loop with Artistic Wire (see p. 77 for instructions).
- Rose quartz bead
- Seed bead
- a

Keyword 6
LEATHER CORD

We used leather cord, combined with natural stones, to make chokers with a look that is natural without being overly casual.

Moonstone Leaf Choker

This choker features a double length of leather cord on which leaf-shaped moonstone beads and freshwater pearl beads are strung. The coloration of the moonstone beads creates an opalescent effect.

Instructions: p. 60

Branch Choker

Metal leaf beads and gemstone-bead nuts hang from a leather cord branch. The turquoise bead adds interest.

Instructions: p. 60

Twist Choker

To make this piece, you simply string beads and wind them around leather cord. The resulting choker has a look that is complex and classic at the same time.

Instructions: p. 61

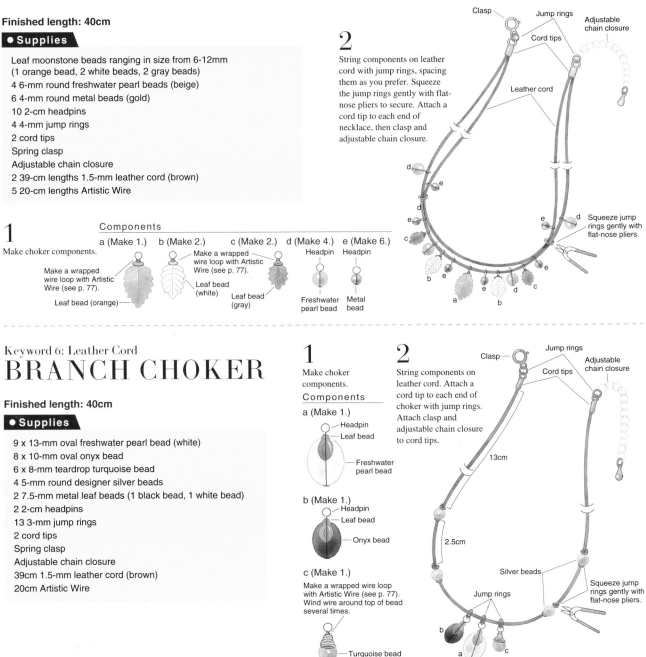

Keyword 6: Leather Cord
MOONSTONE LEAF CHOKER

Finished length: 40cm

● Supplies

Leaf moonstone beads ranging in size from 6-12mm
(1 orange bead, 2 white beads, 2 gray beads)
4 6-mm round freshwater pearl beads (beige)
6 4-mm round metal beads (gold)
10 2-cm headpins
4 4-mm jump rings
2 cord tips
Spring clasp
Adjustable chain closure
2 39-cm lengths 1.5-mm leather cord (brown)
5 20-cm lengths Artistic Wire

1 Make choker components.

Components

a (Make 1.)
Make a wrapped wire loop with Artistic Wire (see p. 77).
Leaf bead (orange)

b (Make 2.)
Make a wrapped wire loop with Artistic Wire (see p. 77).
Leaf bead (white)

c (Make 2.)
Leaf bead (gray)

d (Make 4.)
Headpin
Freshwater pearl bead

e (Make 6.)
Headpin
Metal bead

2 String components on leather cord with jump rings, spacing them as you prefer. Squeeze the jump rings gently with flat-nose pliers to secure. Attach a cord tip to each end of necklace, then clasp and adjustable chain closure.

Clasp   Jump rings   Adjustable chain closure   Cord tips   Leather cord

Squeeze jump rings gently with flat-nose pliers.

Keyword 6: Leather Cord
BRANCH CHOKER

Finished length: 40cm

● Supplies

9 x 13-mm oval freshwater pearl bead (white)
8 x 10-mm oval onyx bead
6 x 8-mm teardrop turquoise bead
4 5-mm round designer silver beads
2 7.5-mm metal leaf beads (1 black bead, 1 white bead)
2 2-cm headpins
13 3-mm jump rings
2 cord tips
Spring clasp
Adjustable chain closure
39cm 1.5-mm leather cord (brown)
20cm Artistic Wire

1 Make choker components.

Components

a (Make 1.)
Headpin
Leaf bead
Freshwater pearl bead

b (Make 1.)
Headpin
Leaf bead
Onyx bead

c (Make 1.)
Make a wrapped wire loop with Artistic Wire (see p. 77). Wind wire around top of bead several times.
Turquoise bead

2 String components on leather cord. Attach a cord tip to each end of choker with jump rings. Attach clasp and adjustable chain closure to cord tips.

Clasp   Jump rings   Adjustable chain closure   Cord tips

13cm

2.5cm

Silver beads

Jump rings

Squeeze jump rings gently with flat-nose pliers.

TWIST CHOKER

Finished length: 40cm

● Supplies

- 6 6-mm round red agate beads
- 6 4-mm round gold sandstone beads
- 6 6-mm round freshwater pearl beads (beige)
- 6 4-mm potato-shaped freshwater pearl beads (gold)
- 6 4-mm round fire-polished beads (crystal copper L)
- 6 6-mm button Swarovski crystal beads (light Colorado topaz)
- 121 1.6-mm 3-cut beads (brown: T CRS460)
- 2 crimp beads
- 2 4-mm jump rings
- 2 cord tips
- Spring clasp
- Adjustable chain closure
- 39cm 1.5-mm leather cord
- 100cm nylon thread

1

Tape nylon thread down to work surface 10cm from end. String beads, referring to patterns in drawings. After working 6 repetitions, tape other end of thread down to work surface.

Patterns

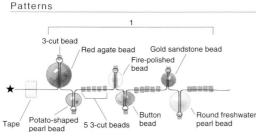

1

3-cut bead — Red agate bead — Gold sandstone bead — Fire-polished bead — Tape — Potato-shaped pearl bead — 5 3-cut beads — Button bead — Round freshwater pearl bead

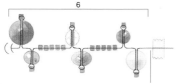

6

Don't add 5 3-cut beads on 6th repetition.

2

String a crimp bead, around which nylon thread has been wound three times, on leather cord 13cm from end. Squeeze crimp bead gently with flat-nose pliers. Apply glue between crimp bead and cord.

Wind thread around crimp bead 3 times. — 13cm — Flat-nose pliers — Crimp bead — Leather cord

3

Wrap beads strung in Step 1 around leather cord, referring to drawing. Attach a crimp bead on opposite side, as in Step 2. Attach cord tips to ends of necklace. Attach clasp and adjustable chain closure to cord tips with jump rings.

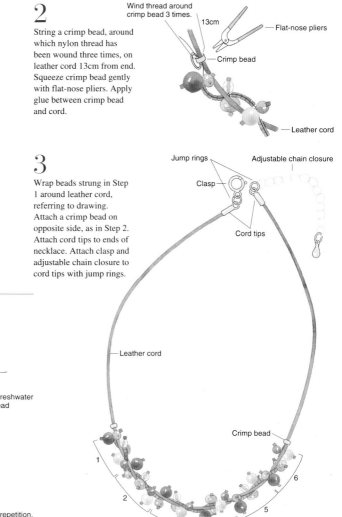

Jump rings — Adjustable chain closure — Clasp — Cord tips — Leather cord — Crimp bead

Working with leather cord

Generally, when you make a choker or bracelet with leather cord, you attach cord tips to the ends, and then clasps or other closures. First, make sure you've cut the cord to the right length. Choose cord tips that will fit the leather cord you're using. Check to ensure that the cord doesn't slip when you're attaching the cord tips.

Attaching a cord tip

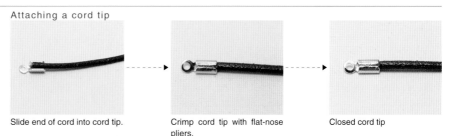

Slide end of cord into cord tip. → Crimp cord tip with flat-nose pliers. → Closed cord tip

Keyword 7
CHAIN

Chain is used so often to make necklaces, but it makes wonderful fringe, too.
Use several different lengths to achieve a good balance.

Long Tassel Necklace

Here we gathered chain and gemstone bead tassels into a
bead cap for a luxuriant look. The necklace features the
same beads as the tassels.

Instructions: p. 65

Swinging Necklace

We used four lengths of chain to create fringe for this
gorgeous necklace with a vintage twist. The teardrop
gemstone beads make for a beautiful balance.

Instructions: p. 64

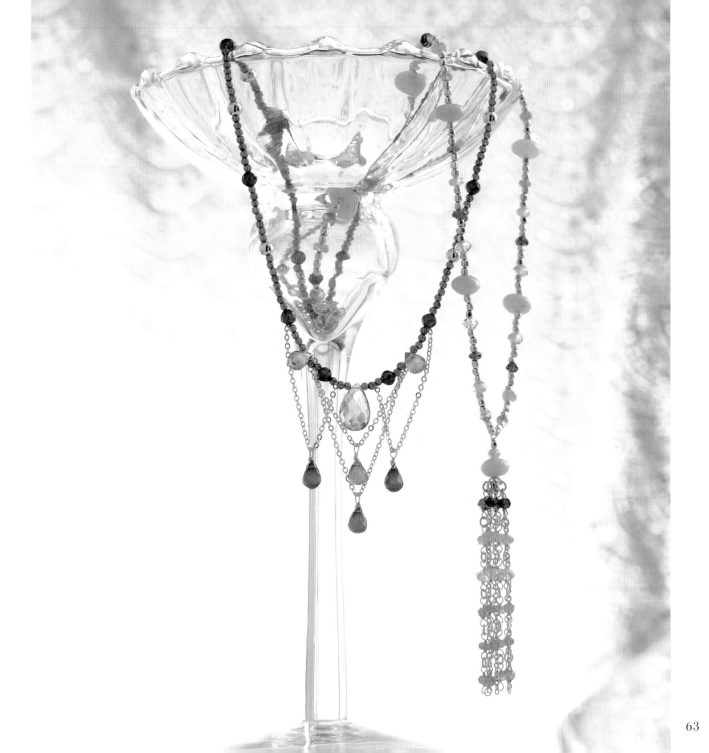

SWINGING NECKLACE

Finished length: 40cm

● Supplies

6 5 x 7-mm teardrop hessonite garnet beads
Round garnet beads (162 2-mm beads, 12 4-mm beads)
10-mm teardrop citrine bead
8 4-mm round metal beads (gold)
2 crimp beads
Chain (3 5.5-cm lengths, 1 8-cm length)
Spring clasp
Adjustable chain closure
4 20-cm lengths Artistic Wire
60cm nylon-coated wire

1

Make necklace components.

Components

a (Make 4.)

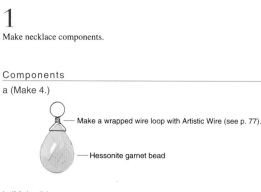

— Make a wrapped wire loop with Artistic Wire (see p. 77).

— Hessonite garnet bead

b (Make 3.)

5.5cm chain

c (Make 1.)

8cm chain

Pattern

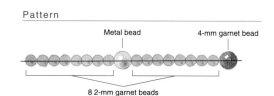

Metal bead

4-mm garnet bead

8 2-mm garnet beads

2

String components and beads on nylon-coated wire. Add a crimp bead at each end of necklace. Attach clasp to one end and adjustable chain closure to other.

Note: Stringing beads and components from one end of the wire will make your work easier.

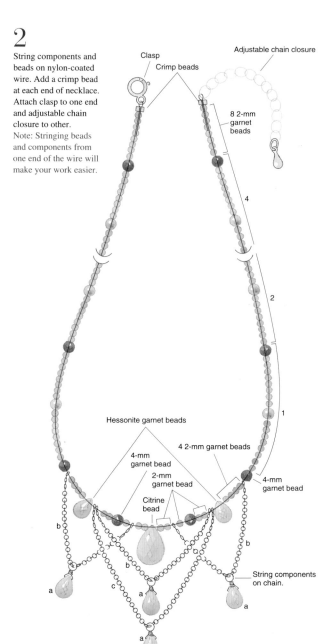

Clasp

Crimp beads

Adjustable chain closure

8 2-mm garnet beads

4

2

1

Hessonite garnet beads

4-mm garnet bead

2-mm garnet bead

Citrine bead

4 2-mm garnet beads

4-mm garnet bead

String components on chain.

LONG TASSEL NECKLACE

Finished length: 46cm
Motif length: 6cm

● Supplies

9 5 x 8-mm button pink opal beads
14 4-mm button garnet beads
14 4-mm button chrysoberyl cat's-eye beads
14 4-mm button citrine beads
23 4-mm button sunstone beads
151 2-mm metal beads (gold)
2 crimp beads
27 3-mm jump rings
4-mm bead cap
3 5.5-cm lengths chain
Spring clasp
Adjustable chain closure
25 20-cm lengths Artistic Wire
80cm nylon-coated wire

1

Make necklace components.

Components

a (Make 4.)

Wrap Artistic Wire around bead with round-nose pliers to form a circle.
Garnet bead

b (Make 4.)

— Chrysoberyl cat's-eye bead

c (Make 4.)

— Citrine bead

d (Make 12.)

— Sunstone bead

e (Make 3.)

5.5cm chain

2

String bead cap and beads on Artistic Wire to make motif. Join bead cap to components made in Step 1 with jump rings.

Metal bead
Sunstone bead
Pink opal bead
Bead cap

Form circles with Artistic Wire with round-nose pliers; wrap ends around base of circle.

a
b
c
d
d
d

Jump rings

e e e

3

String motif and beads on nylon-coated wire. Add a crimp bead at each end of necklace. Attach clasp to one end and adjustable chain closure to other.

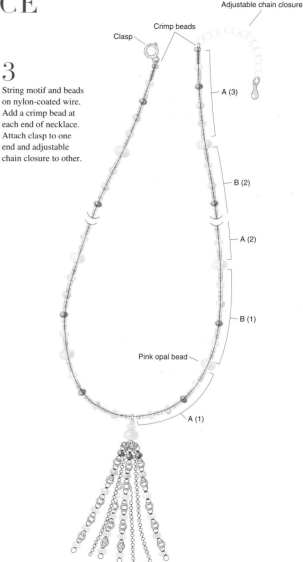

Adjustable chain closure
Clasp
Crimp beads
A (3)
B (2)
A (2)
B (1)
Pink opal bead
A (1)

Patterns

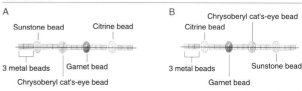

A
Sunstone bead
Citrine bead
3 metal beads
Garnet bead
Chrysoberyl cat's-eye bead

B
Chrysoberyl cat's-eye bead
Citrine bead
3 metal beads
Sunstone bead
Garnet bead

Part 3

SUPER-QUICK, SUPER-EASY DESIGNS

This section features jewelry that you can make quickly and easily by stringing beads or by weaving figure eights. You should be able to finish any one of these pieces in about an hour.

Green & Pink Tablet Necklaces

The focus of these necklaces is the large tablet beads at their centers. The green necklace has an Oriental look to it, while the pink one is delicately charming.

Instructions: p. 68 for green necklace, p. 69 for pink necklace

Pastel Necklace & Earrings

Even bright-colored beads can look sophisticated when combined with paler tones. With their blue lace agate and freshwater pearl bead components, these pieces have a whimsical quality to them.

Instructions: p. 70

Violet Ring

The flower motif is woven with teardrop amethyst beads, among which are strewn sparkling triangle beads and pale blue bicone beads.

Instructions: p. 71

Ring in Shades of Blue

Both the motif and band of this ring are woven on one length of thread. The first and second rows combine to form a three-dimensional shape.

Instructions: p. 71

67

GREEN TABLET NECKLACE

Finished length: 55cm

● Supplies

30 x 40-mm rectangular green aventurine bead
10 6-mm round amber beads
8 oval orange quartz beads ranging in size from 6-10mm
24 2-mm round onyx beads
102 3 x 4-mm top-side-drilled freshwater pearl beads (blue-gray)
4 10-mm octagon glass beads (white opal)
10 8-mm silver designer beads
1 x 2.4-mm metal ring (gold)
4 crimp beads
Spring clasp
Adjustable chain closure
80cm nylon-coated wire

String beads on nylon-coated wire, beginning at center of wire.
Add a crimp bead at each end of necklace.
Attach clasp to one end and adjustable chain closure to other.

Patterns

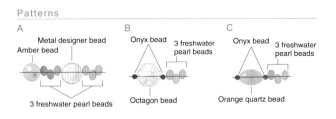

A

Metal designer bead
Amber bead

3 freshwater pearl beads

B

Onyx bead   3 freshwater pearl beads

Octagon bead

C

Onyx bead   3 freshwater pearl beads

Orange quartz bead

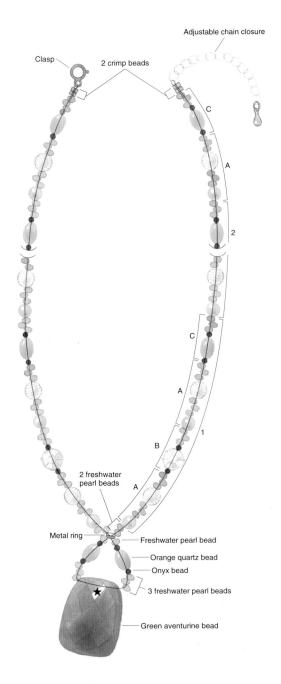

Clasp   2 crimp beads   Adjustable chain closure

C

A

2

C

A

1

B

A

2 freshwater pearl beads

Metal ring   Freshwater pearl bead

Orange quartz bead

Onyx bead

3 freshwater pearl beads

Green aventurine bead

PINK TABLET NECKLACE

Finished length: 55cm

● Supplies (Motif B)

30 x 40-mm rectangular rose quartz bead
Round pink jadeite beads (46 4-mm beads, 3 8-mm beads)
Round onyx beads (46 2-mm beads, 4 4-mm beads)
4 7-mm round coral beads
3 8-mm round mother-of-pearl beads (white)
3 5-mm round turquoise beads
3 6-mm round freshwater pearl beads (green)
24 4-mm bicone Swarovski crystal beads (chalk white)
22 8 x 10-mm cube beads (light green)
1 x 2.4-mm metal ring
20 2-cm headpins
4 crimp beads
Spring clasp
Adjustable chain closure
80cm nylon-coated wire

1

Make necklace components.

Components

a (Make 4.)
○ —Headpin
● —4-mm onyx bead

b (Make 3.)
○ —Headpin
—8-mm pink jadeite bead

c (Make 3.)
○ —Headpin
—Freshwater pearl bead

d (Make 4.)
○ —Headpin
—Coral bead

e (Make 3.)
○ —Headpin
—Mother-of-pearl bead

f (Make 3.)
○ —Headpin
—Turquoise bead

Patterns

A
2-mm onyx bead
4-mm pink jadeite bead
Bicone bead
a
Cube bead

B
b

C
c

D
d

E
e

F
f

Bead arrangement is the same in A-F.

2

String components and beads on nylon-coated wire, creating patterns shown in chart. Add a crimp bead at each end of necklace. Attach clasp to one end and adjustable chain closure to other.

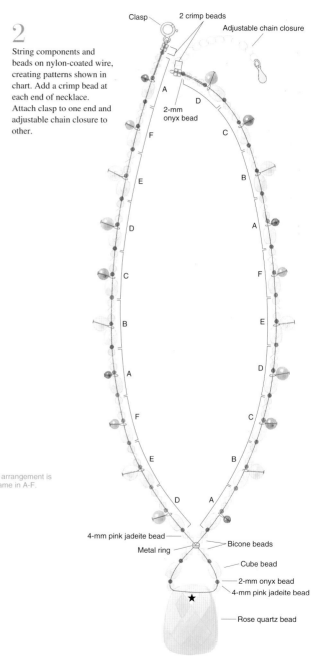

Clasp
2 crimp beads
Adjustable chain closure
2-mm onyx bead

4-mm pink jadeite bead
Metal ring
Bicone beads
Cube bead
2-mm onyx bead
4-mm pink jadeite bead
Rose quartz bead

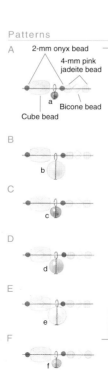

69

PASTEL NECKLACE & EARRINGS

Finished length (necklace): 41cm

● Supplies (Necklace)

3 8 x 10-mm teardrop yellow jade beads
22 4-mm chip amethyst beads
20 4-mm round blue lace agate beads
Brown round mother-of-pearl beads (16 2-mm beads, 24 3-mm beads)
16 2-mm round amazonite beads
22 3-mm bicone Swarovski crystal beads (light azore)
24 4-mm bicone Swarovski crystal beads (Pacific opal)
20 2-mm round metal beads (gold)
12 2-cm headpins
2 crimp beads
Spring clasp
Adjustable chain closure
3 20-cm lengths Artistic Wire
60cm nylon-coated wire

1

Make necklace components.

Components

a (Make 3.)

Make a wrapped wire loop with Artistic Wire (see p. 77).

Yellow jade bead

b (Make 4.)

Headpin

Metal bead

Blue lace agate bead

c (Make 4.)

Headpin

3-mm mother-of-pearl bead

d (Make 4.)

Headpin

4-mm bicone bead

2

String components and beads on nylon-coated wire, making left and right sides in mirror image. Add a crimp bead at each end of necklace. Attach clasp to one end and adjustable chain closure to other.

Pattern

Amethyst bead
Blue lace agate bead
4-mm bicone bead
Metal bead
3-mm bicone bead
Amazonite bead
3-mm mother-of-pearl bead
2-mm mother-of-pearl bead

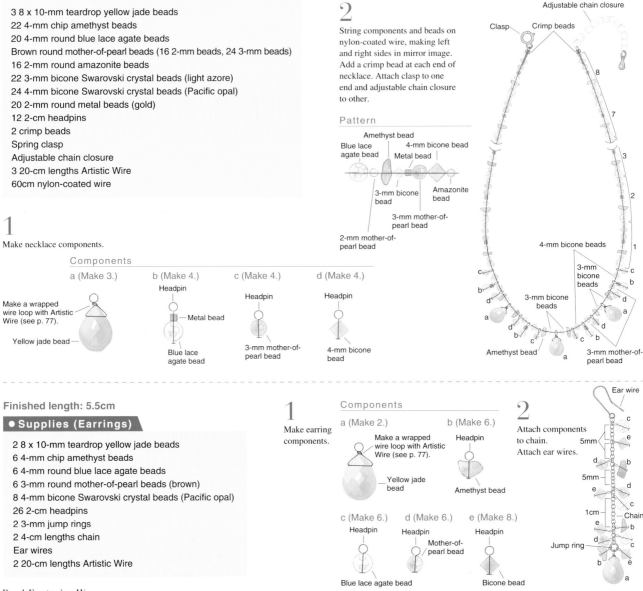

Adjustable chain closure
Clasp
Crimp beads

4-mm bicone beads
3-mm bicone beads
3-mm bicone beads
Amethyst bead
3-mm mother-of-pearl bead

Finished length: 5.5cm

● Supplies (Earrings)

2 8 x 10-mm teardrop yellow jade beads
6 4-mm chip amethyst beads
6 4-mm round blue lace agate beads
6 3-mm round mother-of-pearl beads (brown)
8 4-mm bicone Swarovski crystal beads (Pacific opal)
26 2-cm headpins
2 3-mm jump rings
2 4-cm lengths chain
Ear wires
2 20-cm lengths Artistic Wire

1

Make earring components.

Components

a (Make 2.)

Make a wrapped wire loop with Artistic Wire (see p. 77).

Yellow jade bead

b (Make 6.)

Headpin

Amethyst bead

c (Make 6.)

Headpin

Blue lace agate bead

d (Make 6.)

Headpin

Mother-of-pearl bead

e (Make 8.)

Headpin

Bicone bead

2

Attach components to chain. Attach ear wires.

Ear wire
5mm
5mm
1cm
Chain
Jump ring

VIOLET RING

Approximate size: 6 2 (US)
Motif diameter: 2cm

● Supplies

12 4.5 x 8-mm teardrop amethyst beads
4 3-mm bicone Swarovski crystal beads (Pacific opal)
4 4-mm bicone Swarovski crystal beads (Pacific opal)
7 2.5-mm triangle beads (yellow: M TR1126)
48 2-mm round mother-of-pearl beads (brown)
Nylon thread (1 50-cm length, 1 80-cm length)

1

Make motif, using
80cm nylon thread.

Amethyst bead

★

Triangle bead

2

Add more beads, picking up triangle beads
strung in Step 1. Run thread through 4-mm
bicone beads. Tie threads together.

3-mm bicone bead

Amethyst bead

4-mm bicone bead

3

Pick up a 4-mm bicone bead on motif
with 50cm nylon thread and make band.
Tie threads together and finish off.

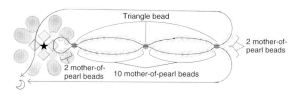

Triangle bead

★

2 mother-of-pearl beads

2 mother-of-pearl beads

10 mother-of-pearl beads

2 mother-of-pearl beads

RING IN SHADES OF BLUE

Approximate size: 6 2 (American)

● Supplies (Necklace)

36 3-mm chip tanzanite beads
8 3-mm button apatite beads
3-mm bicone Swarovski crystal beads
(4 violet beads, 4 violet opal beads, 16 light azore beads)
63 2-mm seed beads (silver: M1)
100cm nylon thread

1

String beads on nylon thread, beginning at center of
thread and weaving figure eights as you go along.

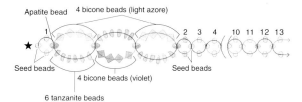

Apatite bead

4 bicone beads (light azore)

1   2 3 4   10 11 12 13

★

Seed beads

Seed beads

4 bicone beads (violet)

6 tanzanite beads

2

Run bottom row through circles of beads woven in Step 1 as you work.
Tie threads to close circle and finish off.

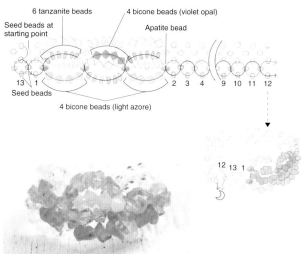

6 tanzanite beads

4 bicone beads (violet opal)

Seed beads at
starting point

Apatite bead

13 1

Seed beads

2 3 4   9 10 11 12

4 bicone beads (light azore)

12 13 1

Snowflake Necklace

This elegant asymmetrical necklace, made with two types of silver beads, is adorned with three bead snowflakes.

Instructions: p. 73

Sunstone Ring

To make this lovely ring, button sunstone beads and smoky quartz beads are woven in a figure-eight pattern, with 3-cut bead accents.

Instructions: p. 74

Swan Ring

The juxtaposition of different beads in this ring, and the purity of the white beads, add up to a very striking piece of jewelry.

Instructions: p. 74

Twin Flower Ring

Worn together, the red ring and the orange-and-yellow ring look like a tiny bouquet of flowers.

Instructions: p. 75

SNOWFLAKE NECKLACE

Finished length: 42cm
Small motif diameter: 1cm
Large motif diameter: 2cm

● Supplies

10 x 11-mm teardrop glass bead (white opal)
Round silver beads (44 2-mm beads, 48 2.5-mm beads)
44 7-mm bugle beads (silver)
3 4-mm round metal beads (gold)
2 crimp beads
2 3-mm jump rings
Spring clasp
Adjustable chain closure
20cm Artistic Wire
Nylon thread (2 40-cm lengths, 1 70-cm length)
60cm nylon-coated wire

1

Make large motif. String
a jump ring on center of
70cm nylon thread, then
add beads, weaving figure
eights.

2.5-mm silver beads

★ Jump ring

2

When you've completed one round, pass
thread through metal bead at center.
Tie threads. Attach teardrop glass bead
component to jump ring.

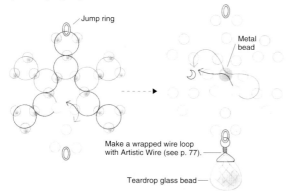

Jump ring

Metal bead

Make a wrapped wire loop
with Artistic Wire (see p. 77).

Teardrop glass bead

3

Make two small motifs, using
40cm nylon thread for each.

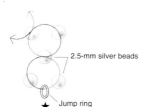

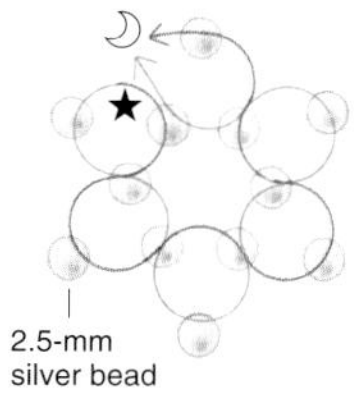

★

2.5-mm
silver bead

4

String motifs and beads on
nylon-coated wire. Add a
crimp bead at each end of
necklace. Attach clasp to
one end and adjustable
chain closure to other.

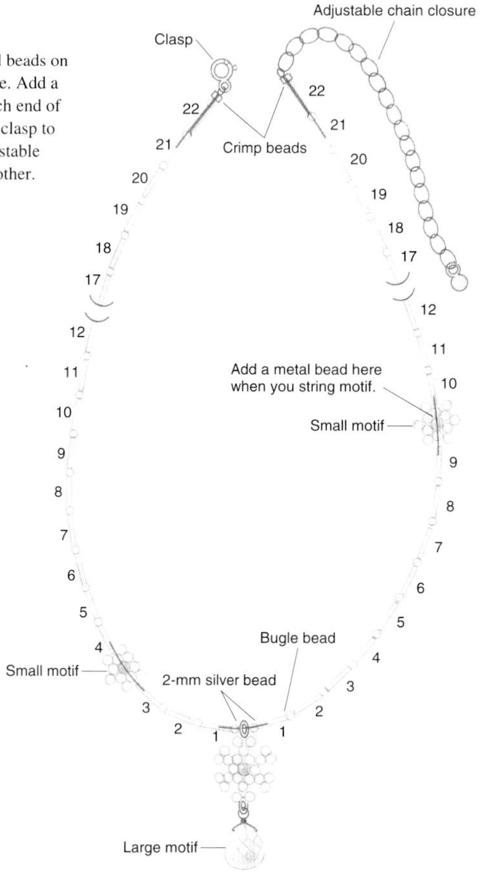

Clasp

Adjustable chain closure

Crimp beads

Add a metal bead here
when you string motif.

Small motif

Small motif

2-mm silver bead

Bugle bead

Large motif

73

Super-Quick, Super-Easy Designs
SUNSTONE RING

Approximate size: 6 (US)

● Supplies

13 4 x 6-mm button sunstone beads
30 2.5-mm round smoky quartz beads
53 2-mm 3-cut beads (gold: T CR712)
90cm nylon thread

1

String beads, weaving figure eights as you
go, and beginning at center of nylon thread.
Set one end of thread aside.

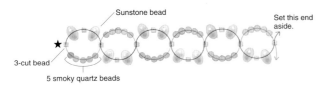

Sunstone bead

Set this
aside.

3-cut bead

5 smoky quartz beads

2

String 8 new 3-cut beads on one end
of thread, picking up 3-cut beads
strung in Step 1 as you go along.
Add a sunstone bead.

Sunstone bead

8 3-cut beads

3

Pass thread through
first 3-cut bead strung,
then into last sunstone
bead strung in Step 2.
Tie thread to end set
aside in Step 1.

Close circle so that 3-cut beads strung in Step 2 lie inside it.

3-cut bead at starting point

Super-Quick, Super-Easy Designs
SWAN RING

Approximate size: 5 2 (US)

● Supplies

3 5 x 6.5-mm teardrop moonstone beads
6 4-mm button moonstone beads
3 5 x 6.5-mm teardrop labradorite beads
6 chip mother-of-pearl beads ranging in size from 5-8mm (white)
4 4-mm round freshwater pearl beads (white)
18 2.5-mm round silver beads
3 5-mm flat designer silver beads
80cm nylon thread

2

Pass thread through first bead strung.
Weave second round.

Teardrop moonstone bead
Button moonstone bead
Freshwater pearl bead
Mother-of-pearl bead

3

Remove tape after weaving the third round.
Tie threads together and finish off.

Button moonstone bead
Round silver beads
Button moonstone bead
Mother-of-pearl bead
Teardrop moonstone bead
Mother-of-pearl bead
Labradorite bead

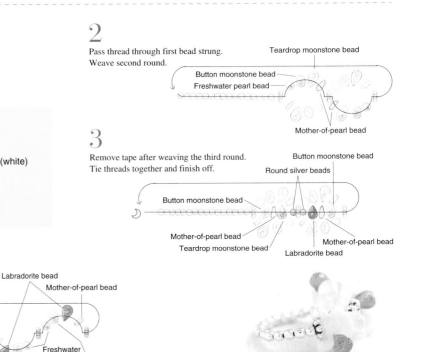

1

Tape nylon thread
down to work surface
20cm from one end.
String beads on thread.

Labradorite bead
Flat silver bead
Mother-of-pearl bead
16 round silver beads
★
Tape
Mother-of pearl bead
Freshwater
pearl beads
Button moonstone beads

TWIN FLOWER RING

Approximate size: 5 2 (US)
Motif diameter: 2cm

6 6 x 8-mm teardrop jade beads (red)
4.5-mm round freshwater pearl bead (white)
20 3-mm round fire-polished beads (bronze)
4-mm fire-polished bead (bronze)
66 1.5-mm seed beads (bronze: T221)
2 60-cm lengths nylon thread

Approximate size: 5 2 (US)
Motif diameter: 1cm

4 5 x 6-mm teardrop olive quartz beads
4 5 x 6-mm teardrop red aventurine beads
2 3-mm round freshwater pearl beads (white)
21 3-mm round fire-polished beads (bronze)
66 1.5-mm seed beads (bronze: T221)
3 60-cm lengths nylon thread

1

String beads on center of nylon thread.

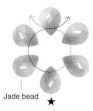

Jade bead ★

2

After weaving one round of figure eights, run thread through beads on perimeter once more. Tie threads together and finish off.

3 seed beads
Seed bead

3

String a freshwater pearl bead on the center of other length of nylon thread. Form an intersection in 4-mm fire-polished bead at back of motif.

★
Freshwater pearl bead

4-mm fire-polished bead

4

Weave band with same length of thread. Tie threads together and finish off.

3-mm fire-polished bead

1 2 3 4   18 19 20 21

Seed bead

1

Weave motif. Tie threads together and finish off. Weave red aventurine beads in same way.

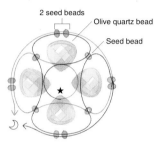

2 seed beads
Olive quartz bead
Seed bead

2

Weave band with a new length of thread, attaching motifs made in Step 1 and freshwater pearl beads midway. Tie threads together and finish off.

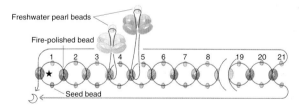

Freshwater pearl beads
Fire-polished bead

1 2 3 4 5 6 7 8   19 20 21

Seed bead

BASIC TECHNIQUES

On the next few pages, we introduce basic
techniques required to make the jewelry in this book,
as well as tips on working with findings.

Weaving figure eights with nylon thread

   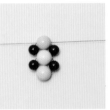

1. String 3 beads on center of thread.

2. Add another bead. Form an intersection in that bead (pass right-hand end of thread through to left, and left-hand end of thread through to right).

3. Add a bead to each end of thread, next to blue bead.

4. Add another bead and form an intersection in it.

5. Pull both ends of thread. Repeat these 5 steps.

Tying and finishing off threads

  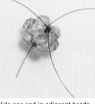  

1. Tie two ends of thread together.

2. Tie ends 1-2 more times for a secure knot.

3. Hide one end in adjacent beads.

4. Pull thread end so that knot slips inside adjacent bead.

5. Cut excess thread at the edge of a bead.

Attaching a spring clasp with a crimp bead

  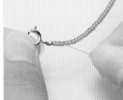  

1. String a crimp bead, then a spring clasp on end of nylon-coated wire.

2. Pass end of wire back through crimp bead and 2 additional beads, forming a circle.

3. Pull end of wire.

4. Compress crimp bead with flat-nose pliers.

5. Finish off by cutting excess wire with wire-cutters. (Attach adjustable chain closures in the same way.)

Joining the halves of a perforated finding

1. Cut tabs on bottom half of finding in half.

2. Bend two adjacent tabs down with flat-nose pliers.

3. Slide top of finding, to which beads have been attached, under bent tabs in bottom.

4. Bend down remaining tabs. Place tissue paper between top and bottom half to prevent damage to thread or beads.

5. Finding with two halves joined

Making a wrapped wire loop

1. Pass Artistic Wire through bead.

2. Wind wire twice around top of bead.

3. Cut one end of wire with wire-cutters.

4. Round other end with round-nose pliers.

5. Wind wire twice around top of bead with your left hand. Cut excess wire.

Rounding ends of pins

1. Insert pin into beads. Cut shaft of pin 7-8mm away from end with wire-cutters.

2. Bend shaft of pin at base of bead to form a right angle with bead.

3. Round end of pin with round nose pliers, beginning at end of shaft.

4. Continue rounding until end of pin is flush with base of bead.

Opening and closing jump rings

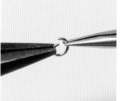

1. Grasp sides of jump ring with flat-nose pliers, and open them by twisting one side toward you and the other away from you.

Joining headpins or eyepins

1. Grasp rounded end of pin with flat-nose pliers, and open it by twisting it gently (from back to front, not sideways).

2. Insert end into other pin.

3. Close circle with pliers.

4. Correctly joined pins

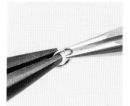

2. Reverse Step 1 to close. For best results, apply equal pressure with left and right hand.

Useful Tools

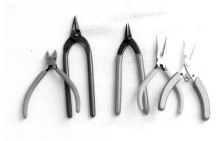

Findings

1. Eyepins: Used to make and connect jewelry components; for the jewelry in this book, we use eyepins that are 0.5-0.6mm thick.
2. Headpins: Also used to make and connect jewelry components. For the jewelry in this book, we use headpins that are 0.5-0.6mm thick.
3. Clasp
4. Adjustable chain closure
5. Spring clasp (often used in combination with an adjustable chain closure).
6. Perforated findings: These are available with and without bar pins attached (see p. 77 for instructions).
7. Earring posts: For the jewelry in this book, we used posts with loops to which beads or other components can be attached.
8. Ear wires

Pliers and cutters

1. Wire-cutters: Used to cut pins and wire.
2. Round-nose pliers: Used to round the ends of headpins and eyepins.
3. Flat-nose pliers: Used to compress crimp beads.
4. Long-nose pliers: Used to open jump rings.
5. Needle-nose pliers

More findings

1. Cord tips: Attached to ends of leather cord and then to a clasp or other closure.
2. Bead caps: Attached to beads with pins to cover beads or add detail.
3. Large jump rings (6mm diameter).
4. Medium jump rings (4mm diameter).
5. Small jump rings (3-3.5mm diameter).
6. Crimp beads: These have several applications, but for the jewelry in this book, they are used to attach nylon-coated wire to a clasp or other closure. We used medium-sized crimp beads (2mm diameter).

Stringing materials

1. Nylon thread: For the jewelry in this book, we used #1.5 (0.205mm diameter) transparent thread.
2. Artistic Wire: Used to make wrapped wire loops; we used wire measuring 0.4-0.6mm in diameter.
3. Nylon-coated wire: Often used to make necklaces; for the jewelry in this book, we used wire measuring 0.24-0.36mm in diameter.

Miscellaneous tools

1. Beading tray: Has a suede lining to keep beads from rolling around.
2. Ring stick: Used to measure ring sizes.
3. Triangular tray: Used to pick up beads from a beading tray.

A selection of Bead work books from J.P.T.

BEAD FANTASIES :
Beautiful, Easy-to-Make Jewelry
by Takako Samejima

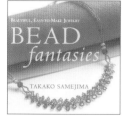

Color photographs of 10 of the 71 pieces include necklaces, bracelets, rings, earrings, brooches, hair ornaments, cell phone straps and eyeglass chains.
66 pages are devoted to brief instructions for the jewelry, supplemented by small color photographs and detailed color drawings. On the last few pages are supplies, and some lessons covering basic bed-stringing, weaving and finishing techniques.

84 pages: 7 1/8 × 7 1/8 in., paperback US$18.00
ISBN 10: 4-88996-128-3   ISBN 13: 978-4-88996-128-7

BEAD FANTASIES II :
More Beautiful, Easy-to-Make Jewelry
by Takako Samejima

With beautiful color photos, detailed drawings and step-by-step instructions, renowned jewelry designer Takako Samejima makes it easy for even the beginner to create eye-catching, original bead accessories. Bead Fantasies II is divided into three sections. The first part focuses on different accessories designed around one motif, for example a clover, a Diamond-shaped flower, a crown. The second section offers patterns that allow readers to use their own beads to create completely original pieces. The third part, entitled "Bead Items" is organized by type of accessory-rings, earrings, bracelets, necklaces and brooches.

84 pages: 7 1/8 × 7 1/8 in, paperback US$18.00
ISBN 10: 4-88996-188-7   ISBN 13: 978-4-88996-188-1

BEAD FANTASIES III :
Still More Beautiful, Easy-to-Make Jewelry
by Takako Samejima

This is the third book of Samejima Takako. This book brings us more of Ms.Samejima's breathtakingly beautiful designs, plus step-by-step instructions for making them. Perhaps beacuse the author has drawn her inspiration from Nature, these stunning designs feature natural materials, such as gemstones and freshwater pearls.

80 pp., 7 7/8 × 7 7/8 in., fully illustrated, paperback US$18.00
ISBN-10: 4-88996-198-4   ISBN-13: 978-4-88996-198-0

BEAD FLOWERS
by Minako Shimonagase

Learn to make exquisite flower creations using simple beads With easy-to-follow instructions and colorful drawings and pictures, Bread Flowers guides readers through the basics, then goes on to offer instructions for creating festive arrangements for special events and occasions, including wedding bouquets, fruits and vegetables for Halloween decorations, Christmas trees and seasonal wreaths.

96 pp., 8 1/4 × 10 1/4 in., 71 pp. color, 25 b/w pages, paperback US$17.95
ISBN 10: 4-88996-190-9   ISBN 13: 978-4-88996-190-4

LOVE and BEADS
By Emi Takamatsu

Tokyo jewelry artist Emi Takamatsu specializes in making hip wearable jewelry and accessories. Her two shops are filled with colorful beads and are a destination place for many young artists. Love and Beads is her first book to be published in English and is a stunning a collection of her original designs featuring Swarovski crystal beads－well-known for their clean lines, elegance, and quality.

64 pp., 8 1/4 × 10 1/8 in., 32 pp. color, 32 b/w pages, paperback. US$12.95
ISBN-10: 4-88996-185-2   ISBN-13: 978-4-88996-185-0

BEADER'S PALETTE

With examples of designs both daring and refined, This book shows how beads of standard sizes and shapes can be combined in dramatic way. With detailed drawings, complete introductions and material guide, it's the perfect guide to learning to make dozens of wearable accessories.

96 pages: 8 1/4 × 10 1/8 in., 46 full color pages, 32 illstrations, .paperback US$19.00
ISBN 10: 4-88996-097-X   ISBN 13: 978-4-88996-097-6

SAMEJIMA Takako
Jewelry designer

Born in Tokyo in 1970, Ms. Samejima has been fascinated by beads since her elementary school days. Her introduction to beads was through craft books, but she is largely self-taught. She had been creating bead jewelry for many years in her spare time, but the demand for her work grew so great that she opened a studio (Crystalloid) in 1995. Since then, she has been a full-time jewelry designer. Her sophisticated pieces, with their masterful use of color, have been featured in many fashion magazines. She is also the author of My Beaded Accessories, Sweet Bead Collection, Pure Beads and Bead Box, all issued by Nihon Bungeisha. English translations of Bead Fantasies 1, 2 and 3 have increased her already wide audience.